MW00613692

the ART of effective living

GARY G. TAYLOR, Ph.D.

Bookcraft
Salt Lake City, Utah

Library of Congress Catalog Card Number: 80:65246
ISBN O-88494-403-4

First Printing, 1980

Lithographed in the United States of America
PUBLISHERS PRESS
Salt Lake City, Utah

Contents

	Acknowledgments	vii
	Introduction	1
1	Don't Make a Problem Out of Striving for Perfection	7
2	Reasonable Responsibility	19
3	It Makes Me Mad	28
4	Guilt and the "I Have To's"	46
5	Reducing Problems by Reducing Stress	61
6	I Really Should Do That, But. . .	74
7	Assertively Avoiding Problems Rather Than Creating Them	89
8	It Works Only if You Work	103
9	Emotional Control Exercises	112
	Index	129

Acknowledgments

My thanks go to the hundreds of clients who have shared their thoughts, emotions, and problems with me during their reach for greater personal and emotional strength. Although names and situations have been modified to protect anonymity, many of their stories illustrate the concepts in this book.

I am also indebted to a capable editor, typist, and concept consultant — my wife. To Susan, a deep sense of gratitude for this service and for the great companion she is in general.

Also, I appreciate Dr. John Fishbein for the ideas he has shared during many fruitful hours of discussion.

Introduction

The scriptures tell us that before we came here we shouted for joy at the prospect. Now that we are here, it is tempting to wonder what all of the shouting was about. When we are caught up in life's complexities, it is easy to forget our eternal destiny and to become embroiled in the problems of living.

Look around. Everyone's life involves a few problems, which isn't surprising if we understand that life is intended to be a learning experience. After all, we wouldn't think of going to school without taking a course or two. It does seem, however, that some people have more than their share of difficulties. Have you ever noticed that some individuals stumble from one catastrophe to another, while others seem to have smooth sailing?

One reason for this is circumstance. Not everyone has the same curriculum in life, although we all share certain basic courses. Another, and I believe more important, reason is that we all have different coping skills. What merely annoys one person can result in deep depression in another; or what annoys a person at one point in his life might be easily passed off at another time.

As the following illustrations show, each inadequate response to life creates several more problems with which we then must deal. As you will notice, ineffective coping skills result both in more problems and in a reduced capacity to deal with them.

Example 1

Mary has been having one of "those days" common for a young mother. Amy has been into *everything* at least three times, and soon the other children will be home from school. The behavior of one active two-year-old is in itself one of life's difficulties, but Mary compounds it. She assumes that if she were an effective mother she would have more control over Amy. After all, look at how well mannered Sister Wilson's children are.

Thus, a second problem has been created. Mary feels inadequate as a mother. Mary also assumes that she must keep the house spotless in order to earn the respect of her mother, her husband, her neighbors, her friends, her visiting teachers, her Father in Heaven, and herself.

Since Amy is not cooperating, a third problem has been created. Mary must keep her house clean, but she cannot because Amy won't cooperate. Now Mary is caught like a nut in a cracker between what she *must* do but simply *cannot* do. Of course, she "could" do it if she (1) were better organized, or (2) had more energy—like Sister Wilson. These thoughts further reduce Mary's self-esteem.

Her normal irritation over Amy's behavior now increases to low-level frustration, anger, and depression. Problems are certainly multiplying for Mary, but the day is yet young. Being somewhat aggravated, Mary naturally has less patience with some of the normal but irritating features of family life. As the children come home from school, the noise level increases, requests for attention are made, a quarrel or two between siblings develops, and the proverbial "Mom, Greg hit me" is heard. Her reduced patience results in Mary's resenting her children (a fourth problem), and in being less temperate than usual with them. The children quickly recognize mom's mood and either get more upset than normal or decide to take advantage of mom's emotional situation by irritating her even further. Their increasingly negative behavior becomes a fifth difficulty for Mary.

The sixth problem walks through the door about 6:30 P.M. asking why dinner isn't ready and why the house is such a mess today, and stating once again how nice it would be to be able to stay home all day and not have to work! In response to this insensitive comment, Mary attacks with vengeance (very unkind language), telling her husband how inconsiderate he is, how hard done by she is, and how her life could be happier if he would only cooperate, etc.

A seventh, eighth, and ninth problem have then been created. Mary and her husband are not speaking to each other for the rest of the evening, which deprives Mary of her husband's support and understanding. Mary feels guilty about some of the nasty things she said in anger that she really didn't mean. In addition, Mary has created a situation in which she can feel better only if her husband behaves in a certain way. It is a serious error to turn our feelings over to the control of others.

Obviously, Mary compounded an unpleasant situation by normal (human), but less than ideal, responses. Each inadequate response created another problem at the same time that Mary's power to cope was being depleted. (Help for the Marys of the world — all of us at one time or another — can be found in subsequent chapters.)

Example 2

Tom prides himself on how well he keeps up the things he owns. He is especially proud of his expensive stereo system, meticulously built up over several years at some financial sacrifice. On returning home from work one evening, he has an uncomfortable feeling that something is wrong, followed almost immediately by a sick feeling in his stomach as he realizes that the stereo is missing. As he looks around, he sees that his home has been burglarized. His stereo, television, and a shotgun are gone. Tom has been victimized. Nobody has a right to take what doesn't belong to him. Tom has worked for his possessions, and he and his family are the only ones with a legitimate right to use them.

Suppose, however, that Tom becomes exceptionally angry as he surveys his loss. In fact, Tom gets so angry that he slams his fist into the wall. Two new problems have just been created. There is now an unsightly hole in the wall that needs to be patched, and Tom's hand hurts. In his anger Tom yells at his wife on her return home. "If you hadn't been off playing tennis" (selfishly he implies), "this wouldn't have happened." The logic of the statement escapes Tom's wife, and thus a temporary problem is created in Tom's marriage.

Suppose further that Tom has an idea that a neighbor down the street was responsible for the burglary. A little investigation actually confirms the suspicion. Tom lets himself into the neighbor's garage and discovers his property under cover in the corner. Rather than being relieved that he has located his property and calling the police, Tom arms himself and angrily confronts the neighbor. A scuffle ensues, and Tom shoots the burglar. Some might argue that it served the burglar right, but Tom will have a difficult time convincing a jury that his response was morally justified. Tom's inadequate coping response has created some major difficulties in his life. He faces court costs, lost employment, guilt because of his overreaction, possible imprisonment, and disturbance in his family relationships.

These hypothetical cases are related to countless real-life instances in which individuals compound situations by their reaction to ordinary problems. A San Diego paper reported an instance in which a young child took a hammer to the fiberglass body of his father's Corvette. The father became so angry when he observed the damage that he took the same hammer to his boy's hands. The boy's later question, "If I promise not to do it again can I have my hands back?" and the biting guilt over his own behavior may haunt that father for years. Dan White, a former County Supervisor in San Francisco, also knows first-hand how problems multiply. In response to what he considered unfair treatment, Dan White shot to death San Francisco Mayor Moscone and a County Supervisor Harvey Milk. Dan White's life was ruined by this act; and what about the eternal consequences for him?

What can we do to reduce problems in living? Current studies indicate that coping skills may be influenced by body chemistry. For example, hypoglycemia, food additives, menstrual cycles, and other physiological variables have been correlated with emotional upset. But these studies typically are not definitive, and for every rule there are usually many exceptions. In fact, in my experience, what we *think* is generally at the root of our emotional upset. Often we can learn to deal with life's problems effectively by simply changing some of our attitudes and concepts; and in so doing, we can actually reduce the number of problems we face.

The following chapters discuss coping strategies from the context of the scriptures and of current psychological thinking. Each chapter discusses an important principle that, when implemented, can make your life more comfortable *and productive*. These concepts can be built into your life through a number of exercises described throughout the book. Each of the ideas offered in the following chapters is based on the premise that the gospel of Jesus Christ is the foundation for both temporal and eternal happiness. Obviously, the Savior had more than his share of problems, but he demonstrated effective coping ability throughout his life. Our challenge is to do likewise. As we do so, we establish a basis for happiness here and, at the same time, we better prepare ourselves for the hereafter.

Don't Make a Problem Out of Striving for Perfection

1

Latter-day Saints are a goal-oriented, perfection-bound people. Christ's injunction for us to be perfect is an often-remembered indication that individual perfection is both a celestial requirement and a real possibility. Unfortunately, some of us seem to stumble over this principle rather than find edification in it. When we stumble, it is usually because of one or more of the following *mis*perceptions:

1. Perfection must be achieved immediately.
2. We need to be perfect in everything.
3. Mistakes and perfection are absolutely contradictory concepts.
4. Perfection requires perfectionistic goals.

Perfection Need Not Be Achieved Immediately

Many people quit their celestial pursuit for the same reason that my daughter wanted to quit learning to play the piano — practicing is painful. My daughter felt that learning to play the piano was too difficult. Actually, the problem was not that playing the piano was too difficult, but that she was judging her level of performance against that of others who had already put in years of study and practice. She wanted to take a few lessons and become Primary pianist. It is not only too hard, it is absolutely impossible to learn to play the piano well as a result of just a few lessons. It is also not only too difficult, it is absolutely impossible to become spiritually perfect overnight. Apparently we were preparing for aeons before this mortal existence, and experience tells us that becoming perfect is a slow process while here.

What is needed, of course, is a one-step-at-a-time philosophy. You can learn to play the piano if you continue to practice, moving from one level of expertise to the next. You can become perfect if you continue to try, moving from one degree of progress to the next. The goal at any given point should be the next level, not the final result. Otherwise we tend to be overcome with a sense of hopelessness. From the bottom of the mountain looking up, it seems as if the goal is impossible. Usually we can identify the steps necessary to reach the first plateau, however. And once there, we can have a clearer view of the next step, and so on until we reach the summit. Focusing too intently on the final goal can be depressing unless we are realistic about intermediate steps in the process.

The problem of perfection outlined above can occur in connection with conference sessions, Relief Society meetings, *Ensign* reading, and so forth. I am surprised at the number of people who come away from such spiritual opportunities depressed rather than edified. I know a few bishops who annually prepare for an increase in counseling sessions following Education Week. Conference sessions can also lead to a rash of anxiety attacks. Why? In some cases anxiety is created by a healthy sense of guilt and remorse (see chapter 4). Guilt is appropriate and helpful under many circumstances. In other cases, though, individuals get caught focusing on the goal and not on the steps in the perfection process. They are overwhelmed by a general rather than a specific sense of guilt, which is actually counterproductive to their eternal quest. They become discouraged when they gauge how far they are from the top of the mountain.

Someone once counted the number of directives issued from the pulpit during a stake conference session — something like fifty-eight by the sixth speaker. The directives in total represented a level of performance considerably higher than that of most individuals in the congregation. Rather than let the Spirit direct them regarding where to spend improvement energy most wisely, some considered it their obligation to complete all of the directives immediately. As a result they felt that their present steady efforts were not sufficient, they became unhappy with themselves, and they feared that they would never be good enough to be acceptable to the Lord either. This combination of frustration and self-doubt actually led some to lessen their commitment to the gospel. Others made improvements in their life in the short run, but before long they crashed under the weight of unrealistic expectations.

Expecting to immediately follow all of the directives and complete all of the goals suggested by individuals in Church meetings is like going to a banquet and feeling obligated to eat everything there. Information disseminated in Church meetings is almost always good advice, and much of it is essential to exaltation. But we need to pick and choose improvement goals wisely rather than feel obligated to do everything at once. One-step perfection is a concept championed by Lucifer, who knows that it will eventually lead to emotional upset in those who attempt to practice it, as surely as eating too much food leads to stomach upset.

We Need Not Be Perfect in Everything

It goes without saying that no one has the intellect, stamina, time, or talent to do *everything* well, let alone perfectly. Yet many individuals create within themselves the need to do just that. They want to be perfect in everything right now. We don't even know whether Jesus himself was a flawless carpenter, in the sense that he never made a mistake or failed to do a faultless job, but the concept that he was the only perfect being who ever lived does not require that superhuman technical excellence. There is no record of his being a great artist, chemist, or musician. In fact, there are probably other areas of human endeavor in which the Savior did not make significant contributions — not because he could not have done so, but simply because he had more important things to do. Of course, it is no sin not to be a flawless carpenter or not to be a great artist or musician. The Savior did avoid sin perfectly, and he did live perfectly and complete his mission perfectly — and that's what counted.

Some of us were raised to believe that nothing deserves mediocre effort. "If a job is worth doing, it is worth doing well." That philosophy works fine if you have only one or two relatively simple jobs to do. It leads to procrastination and self-depreciation in the normal situation in which there are more things to do than time allows or in which the skills required to do the job well are beyond us. This philosophy also leads to trouble when it is applied to areas of endeavor that deserve less attention than others.

Take, for example, the role of a homemaker. There is nothing inherently wrong with gourmet meals, spotless floors, and children who look (for a few minutes) as if they had stepped out of a fashion magazine. But there is something wrong if a homemaker feels she can be successful in her role only if she produces gourmet meals, spotless floors, and meticulously groomed children. Although some attention to these matters is obviously important, a family can function beautifully if less than perfect effort is given to meal preparation, cleanup operations, and children's grooming. A homemaker creates a problem if she becomes so frustrated and uptight about less than spotless floors or other household tasks that it disrupts family harmony. Of course, this statement should not be used as a rationalization for inadequate home maintenance (see chapter 6 on procrastination).

Mistakes and Perfection Are Not Necessarily Contradictory Concepts

The only way for a mortal to avoid mistakes is to withdraw from life. Perhaps a hermit sealed off from interaction with others and removed from most of life's responsibilities could exist without making mistakes. But, of course, that kind of life-style itself would be a great mistake. We need to be involved with people and to live life fully because, for one thing, experience is a primary objective of mortality. The avenue to celestial perfection involves living, and there is no way to live without making mistakes. In that sense, mistakes and perfection do not contradict one another. Rather, making mistakes and learning from them are necessary parts of the perfection process.

A life without mistakes, or a life of innocence, is apparently the kind of life lived by Adam and Eve prior to the Fall. But their eternal development depended, as ours does now, on living in a world where mistakes are possible.

> And now, behold, if Adam had not transgressed he would not have fallen, but he would have remained in the garden of Eden. And all things which were created must have remained in the same state in which they were after they were created; and they must have remained forever, and had no end.
>
> And they would have had no children; wherefore they would have remained in a state of innocence, having no joy, for they knew no misery; doing no good, for they knew no sin.
>
> But behold, all things have been done in the wisdom of him who knoweth all things.
>
> Adam fell that men might be; and men are, that they might have joy. (2 Nephi 2:22-25.)

It is hoped that we can learn vicariously many lessons about the consequences of errors and mistakes by observing others. But, inevitably, because we are human, we will make many mistakes ourselves. And as suggested above, for the sake of our eternal goal, we must live in an environment which allows wrong choices and opposition.

A knowledge of this fact is important for those of us who create problems for ourselves by being traumatized when we make mistakes. To condemn and depreciate oneself or another because of a mistake is not unlike condemning and punishing a child who falls down while learning to walk. How can a child learn to walk without falling down a few times? How can a mortal learn to act perfectly without making a few mistakes along the way? A child ridiculed or punished for falling down while learning to walk may still learn to walk, but certainly the natural learning process will be disrupted and learning will take longer than normal.

Punishing ourselves for mistakes has a similar result. Sometimes we are so busy condemning ourselves that we forget to identify the factors leading to the problem, and we fail to recognize the cues or signals which could warn us of danger when a similar problem recurs. Mistakes are a natural part of the perfection process. While we must not be complacent about them, they are to be learned from. In this context, of course, "learning from a mistake" includes earnestly striving not to repeat it. Mistakes are not to be sought after but, because we are human, they are to be viewed as an inevitable part of our human strivings.

This fact we clearly understood in the eternal council prior to mortality. There One stepped forward in support of a plan in which those willing to learn from their mistakes and willing to conform to a few simple regulations would have the consequences of those mistakes forever erased.

What should we do then when we make a mistake? Rather than saying to ourselves, *What a rotten person I am!* our response ought to be, *What can I learn from it? How can I avoid making the same error in the future?* As suggested above, self-condemnation robs us of the motivation to improve, and it also disrupts the learning opportunities provided by mistakes.

Of course, this does not mean that we can ignore the repentance process when we have committed sins. The approach recommended here aids that process. Recognizing the error, feeling sorrow, confessing and forsaking the sin, and seeking forgiveness are all compatible with avoiding self-ridicule. In fact, if we persist in severe self-condemnation we are not as likely to receive the full benefits of the repentance process.

How do we know when we have made a mistake? In spite of the negative consequences, we tend to overreact to mistakes by condemning and ridiculing ourselves rather than to accept mistakes as a natural part of life. It also seems to be a common tendency to assume that we have erred when sometimes we have not. Perfect behavior can be defined only by a perfect standard. The gospel provides such a standard, but the attitudes and impressions of mortals do not. It is a mistake under any circumstance to act dishonestly, immorally, or counter to the gospel standard in any way. But sometimes we evaluate our behavior on the basis of feedback from mortals (an imperfect standard) and end up hanging an innocent person.

For example, Jane felt inadequate as a worker and experienced fairly serious depression over the fact that she wasn't successful at work. But in analyzing the situation, I could clearly see that Jane was a successful worker. She worked hard all day, rarely taking the breaks to which she was entitled (and which probably would have increased her overall work output). Jane seldom reported in sick even when she was ill; and she did her best to work efficiently. She made mistakes on the job (who doesn't), but she made an effort to learn from those mistakes. The problem was not Jane's level of skill or her work habits, but rather that the department in which she worked was poorly managed and understaffed. Jane was required to do more than could reasonably be expected of a worker. Instead of questioning the standard, Jane questioned herself. As a result, she suffered a loss of self-respect and confidence, which in turn led to more mistakes on the job and a more inferior job performance than normal.

As an additional example, many people judge the appropriateness of their social conduct on the basis of the reactions of others. A father assumes he said the wrong thing if his child reacts emotionally. A friend feels guilty if a comment intended to be helpful is reacted to negatively by another. A bishop feels he has made a mistake if his comments cause the person being counseled to burst into tears. In each case what was said may have been entirely appropriate. An emotional response says something about what the receiver is thinking, but it says very little about the appropriateness of the comment itself. Many people reacted emotionally to statements made by the Savior, not because his statements were untrue or inappropriate but simply because the listeners were not ready to accept what he said.

Of course, it is possible (and easy) to make mistakes in interpersonal relations. Inevitably, we do or say inappropriate things at times. Again, the opinion or reaction of others normally is not a good standard against which to evaluate our behavior. The appropriate standard is the gospel. We might ask ourselves, "Was my comment or behavior cruel, intolerant, insensitive, or dishonest?" If so, it was a mistake no matter how the receiver reacted to it. If the comment or behavior was congruent with gospel principles, it was correct no matter how it was received.

Sometimes the input we receive from others can help us in judging the merits of our behavior. But most of the time we pay too much attention to the reaction of others and not enough to the perfect and, therefore, much more reliable standard of gospel principles. This general issue is discussed in more detail in chapter 4.

Ultimate Perfection Does Not Require Interim Perfectionistic Goals

Some of the biggest obstacles blocking our development toward perfection are our bad habits. Most of us at one time or another struggle to eliminate undesirable behavior, such as gossiping, smoking, drinking, taking drugs, overeating, and impure thinking. Our goal is to totally remove such behavior from our lives. But the way we approach the challenge can have a significant impact on the probability of success.

Tom tried everything to quit smoking — everything, that is, but quitting. Everything from being hypnotized to pulling a rubber band against his wrist whenever he thought of smoking did little good. In talking with Tom about the problem, I judged that he was afraid to quit. He was scaring himself with his choice of goals. He would set a goal, such as, "I will never have another cigarette starting Thursday morning." That perfectionistic goal meant that he was always only one step away from failure. If he let down even once, as he always did, he condemned himself as a total failure. He lost faith in himself, and he was even more convinced that he would fail again.

Tom decided to establish the goal of reducing his cigarette intake gradually, rather than to stop cold turkey. As part of the gradual reduction process, he carefully recorded cigarette consumption. Rather than condemning himself when he smoked a cigarette, he simply recorded the incident and asked himself what factors were related to smoking the cigarette. He also thought about how he could avoid smoking the next time a similar incident occurred. Instead of spending energy condemning himself, he spent energy in analyzing the problem and in developing a new strategy for its solution. After this brief analysis, he immediately started again on his goal of reducing smoking. As his faith in himself increased, he was able to reduce intake to the point that smoking was eliminated altogether.

Obviously there are some people who can decide to quit smoking Thursday morning and never again touch a cigarette. But that approach does not work for everyone, unless perhaps (as in the conversion process) they seek the help of the Spirit. A more gradual reduction program with realistic interim goals can help others achieve the same objective. In general, we should insure that our improvement goals are within reach; and we should understand that any effort toward the goal is better than no effort at all. Some people assume that they are total failures if they do not reach their goals immediately; with this attitude they are worse off than when they started. They still have the problem, and in addition they have accompanying guilt feelings. Usually, however, they have made some improvement which is of value whether or not they have reached the final goal.

We Don't Have to Be so Hard on Ourselves

The general concepts presented in this chapter suggest that we should not be so hard on ourselves. This is a frightening thought for many people who have been reared to believe that progress can be made only by putting great pressure on themselves. But a theory used in business and industry applies to our discussion here.

Douglas McGregor coined a set of terms which describe two philosophies of management — Theory X and Theory Y.[1] Theory X, in part, suggests that employees lack ambition, dislike responsibility, prefer to be led, and are self-centered, gullible, and not very bright. Therefore, under Theory X the best way to get people to produce is to overtly manipulate them with either the threat of punishment or the promise of external rewards (carrot-and-stick approach).

Under Theory Y people are assumed *not* to be passive, lazy, indolent, or stupid by nature. They may at times act that way, but under the proper environment their true character will emerge. Theory Y states that people produce more when given responsibility, social support, encouragement, and appreciation. Considerable research and experience suggests that under most circumstances there are far greater benefits in working from Theory Y instead of from Theory X.

As we relate these two theories to everyday behavior, it seems that we often adopt a Theory X posture with ourselves. We assume that we lack self-control, that we are worthless, and

---

[1]Douglas M. McGregor, "The Human Side of Enterprise," in *Studies of Personal and Industrial Psychology,* ed. Edwin A. Fleishman (Homewood, Illinois: Dorsey Press, 1967).

that we must keep a very strong carrot-and-stick perspective if we are ever to become perfect. But it is important, correct, and certainly more effective to remember that we are children of God, that we have perfect eternal parents and infinite potential (Theory Y). While it is true that mortality has created some problems which make it more difficult for our true character to emerge, inside these physical bodies are spirits interested in progress and development.

Rather than being heavy-handed with ourselves, we can often make better time by removing obstacles that hinder natural development. One such obstacle is lack of faith, essentially a fear that we cannot make it. By establishing realistic goals and settling for measured progress we will inevitably develop our faith, although perhaps not at the pace we had hoped for.

This notion can be illustrated using a concept labeled *quasi-stationary equilibrium*.[2] The basic assumption is that our level of output (shown below as good works) is always in a state of flux, suspended between contradicting forces. Some of these forces are indicated in the figure below as they relate to our Church activity. Notice that the factors on the bottom of the line push us to do good works, while those on the top of the line limit productive behavior. Our output of good works at any given time depends on which set of forces is strongest at the moment.

If we want to raise our output of good works, we can either increase the forces on the bottom or decrease the forces on the top. The problem is that if we increase pressure on the bottom, we must maintain that pressure in order to keep production high. The minute we let up on the pressure, our level of good works falls because of the counterforces exerting pressure from the top (e.g., influence of Satan and lack of faith in self). In other words, we can improve our performance by putting pressure on ourselves; but the improvement, which certainly requires considerable effort because of natural or self-created

[2] Mason Haire, *Psychology in Management* (New York: McGraw-Hill, 1964), pp. 162-180.

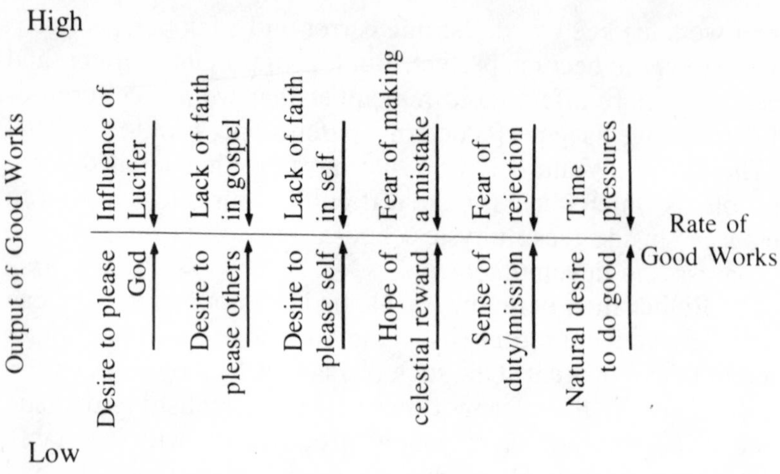

High

Output of Good Works

Forces pushing down ↓	Forces pushing up ↑
Influence of Lucifer	Desire to please God
Lack of faith in gospel	Desire to please others
Lack of faith in self	Desire to please self
Fear of making a mistake	Hope of celestial reward
Fear of rejection	Sense of duty/mission
Time pressures	Natural desire to do good

Rate of Good Works

Low

forces working against us, may be short-lived. In fact, putting more pressure on the bottom usually increases pressure on the top, such as lack of faith in self, weariness, and rebellion.

The other strategy is to work on the natural, self-created forces which are keeping production down. By building faith in God and in ourselves, by overcoming fear of rejection, and by organizing our time, we remove counterpressures and our output of good works floats up, sustained by our natural desires to do good. Approaching self-improvement from this perspective is less costly emotionally and much easier to maintain.

Hints on how to eliminate or reduce some of the forces pushing back our output of good works are provided in subsequent chapters. The major ideas in this chapter show us how we can reduce counterproductive pressures in our life by remembering that (1) perfection need not be achieved immediately; (2) The perfection we are commanded to seek does not require flawless performance in every activity in life; (3) mistakes along the road and ultimate perfection are not contradictory concepts; and (4) ultimate perfection does not require interim goals which are rigidly perfectionistic.

Reasonable Responsibility

2

By design, life presents us with many problems; but we often unnecessarily create even more problems by assuming responsibility for events and circumstances over which we have no control. It is possible to do a great job of organizing a ward activity, even though the result is not a well-run ward social. It is possible to be a near-perfect father and to have misbehaving children. It is possible to be a very good spouse and to have one's marriage end in divorce. Yet all too often we define the adequacy of our performance on the basis of outcome, even when our performance is only one factor in a series of variables affecting that outcome. In fact, it is such a common tendency that initially many readers will probably disagree with the three statements on responsibility given above. Each one, therefore, is repeated below and given supportive rationale.

A good chairman, but a poor activity

John was chairman of the ward activities committee, and his group had been assigned responsibility for a ward dinner. Within a week of having been given the assignment, but only three weeks from the scheduled event, John called his committee together to discuss the matter for the first time. To that first meeting John brought a checklist of all tasks and subtasks necessary to complete the project. Major items, such as publicity, entertainment, food purchase, food preparation, and building setup were included on the checklist as well as specific assignments under each major heading. In addition to John, only two of the three members of the committee attended the meeting, even though all three had promised to attend when contacted a day or two before.

The committee organized a general plan for the event and specific assignments for each committee member. John gave the absent committee member her assignment in person within a day or two and completed his own assignment within a week. John gave himself responsibility for entertainment and arranged for a comedy-song act by a well-known couple in the stake. John also called the other committee members at the end of the week for a status report on their preparations. Each indicated that he or she was working on the assignment and that all was going according to plan.

Most, but not all, preparations went according to plan. The person responsible for food purchase passed around sign-up sheets during ward meetings and purchased food according to the number who indicated they would attend. But the person responsible for building setup waited too long before completing his assignment. As a result, decorations were very modest and a few irritated ward members had to change their plans and set up tables and chairs at the last minute. Also at the last minute John received a call that one of the members of the team who was to provide the entertainment was ill and the other was unable to perform without him. As a *coup de grace*, many more people decided to come to the dinner than had earlier expressed interest, and this resulted in a shortage of food.

The result was a less than well-run ward dinner and a temptation for John to feel unsuccessful. But was he? Getting the assignment too late for adequate planning was not John's fault. John could not prevent the committee member from waiting too long to arrange for building setup. John asked for one status report, and if he had given more direction he would have run the risk of offending the committee member responsible by reassuming assignments he had delegated. Of course, John could not prevent the illness which eliminated the entertainment, and backup plans were not possible given the time constraints. The food situation might have been improved with advance ticket sales or with a more effective interest poll. But again, John had delegated responsibility for the food purchase to someone else; and, in any event, time constraints made anything other than what was done impractical.

In effect, John did the practical things he could to insure a well-run ward dinner. Circumstances beyond his control and human fallibility in others (also beyond his control) led to an outcome not at all indicative of John's efforts.

A near-perfect father can have misbehaving children

The role of father (or mother) is so complex and intertwined with all facets of living that it is as impossible to be a perfect father as it is to be a perfect person. Every father can expect to make mistakes at times. It is frequently difficult for a father to know whether, in the offspring's interest, he should insist on a course of action which overrules his son's or daughter's free agency. It is hard, for instance, to reach a balance between being overprotective and not protective enough. Let us assume however that within the bounds dictated by his humanness, Alan is a near-perfect father. Observers admire his patience; yet he does expect obedience from his children, and he sets down firm but not unrealistic guidelines for their conduct. Alan is also a model of propriety in his own life. He is well respected by his church and community and is one of those individuals who has an almost untiring ability to accomplish good works.

Alan is busy in Church and business affairs, but he also spends time with his family. He regularly conducts family prayer, home evening, and similar activities, and he frequently counsels with his children and spends individual time with each one.

In spite of this, Alan's son Paul is a problem child. Paul was a little hyperactive as he was growing up, but basically he was a good child. Teachers seemed to enjoy him, and he did well in school. Unfortunately, as Paul started junior high school he developed a sullen attitude at home and began to fight against Church attendance and family activities. His friends were not the best influence on him, and it soon became obvious that Paul was dabbling in drugs and alcohol. Attempts by his parents to control the problem by placing Paul on restriction seemed to aggravate the situation even more, to the point that Paul ran away from home when he was fifteen and was arrested for burglary.

What went wrong? Alan began to question his parenting ability: *Maybe I should have been home more. I should have spent more time with Paul. I was probably overly strict, or maybe I wasn't strict enough.* Certainly in recent months Alan had not been as patient with Paul as he might have been. In fact, Alan was reaching the point where it was even difficult for him to like Paul.

But let's look more closely. Alan's impatience came *after,* not before, his son developed problems. Alan's growing intolerance and loss of kind feeling for Paul had not caused Paul's problems. As a matter of fact, whatever went wrong in Paul's life probably was not his father's fault. Alan had set the right example; he had tried to teach and instruct his son. He took every action he could think of to help Paul resolve the problem; and he had taken the matter to the Lord.

If this situation resolves itself as most do, Paul will find himself and yet thank his parents for their effort and concern in his behalf. The good effort given by Alan is likely to be rewarded later in life. But we would do well to remember that children can have problems even when their parents do an excellent job of parenting. Conversely, some children demonstrate remarkable coping ability and make excellent adjustment in spite of poor parenting. One reason for these differences is that parents can influence but cannot control their children's decisions. Other factors, including influence of peers and teachers, and the child's perception and natural ability, play a part in what the child becomes.

This is not to demean the extent of parental influence. It is powerful, and we have a God-given responsibility to teach our children (see D&C 68:25, for example). But we cannot guarantee that our children will develop in the ways we would like them to. A guarantee as to their actions is possible only if the environment is so severely restricted and force so strong that sin is virtually impossible. That sounds too much like a plan vetoed by a wise Father before this world was created. Even if children could be forced to behave, they would not thereby develop self-initiative and self-control, which obviously are basic elements in eternal development. It is possible then to do an admirable job as a parent and yet be disappointed in the outcome of our children.

I suppose our Eternal Father was saddened that a third of his children disobeyed his wishes and forfeited their chance for mortality. Among mortals Lehi is an example of a parent who probably did his job well but was disappointed in the result. Even though our children sometimes make serious mistakes, not many of them plan to murder their brother, as did two of Lehi's sons. This near tragedy occurred in spite of a godly example by their father and much effort and prayer on his part.

A very good spouse, but a very bad marriage

It is as difficult to be a perfect spouse as it is to be a perfect parent or a perfect person. We should not expect to be free of mistakes as marriage partners. Certainly each of us should understand that his or her spouse will make mistakes. Divorce often comes as these mistakes are emphasized and as idealistic expectations develop regarding how much better life could be with another partner. In a general sense it is true that divorce occurs because of failings on the part of both partners, but consider the following examples.

Ann was a convert to the Church of about ten years. She

was a kind, sensitive, and delightful person. Ann has grown to feel good about herself, but early in her life she suffered from self-doubt. It was at that point that she married her husband. She was so unsure of herself and so anxious to leave home that she rushed into a marriage with an immature and emotionally unstable man. Over the years she has been subject to abuse from a critical husband who has taken little interest in the family and no interest in the Church, and who has rarely provided emotional or psychological support for Ann.

After many years of marriage, Ann's husband reported that he was seeing another woman and that he wanted a divorce. Although she had made mistakes and had contributed to the marital discord, Ann was as good a partner as anyone could realistically be. Occasionally she lost her temper, and at times she was critical, unkind, and insensitive. Those, however, usually were instances related to considerable provocation from her husband. In general, she did an admirable job of coping with a difficult situation.

As is often true, though, Ann felt guilty about the divorce. *Perhaps if I had been more kind, Fred would not have left. Maybe if I had been available more often to him sexually, or perhaps I shouldn't have insisted on my right to attend sacrament meeting.* It is always possible to second-guess oneself, but in this case Ann was being a reasonable marriage partner and had tried hard to make the relationship work. We should always be careful to avoid blaming others for our own problems (see chapter 3), but there are times when relationships do not work in spite of our best efforts.

We Are Responsible Only for That Which We Can Control

The examples given above have a common element: individuals striving to do well were handicapped in their effort by the limitations of others. Because many important outcomes in life depend on more than one person or on variables not under an individual's control, it is possible to do our best and still not gain the outcome we desire. This fact leads to the axiom heading this section: We are responsible only for that which we can control.

We can control ourselves, both our feelings and our behavior; but we cannot control the behavior and feelings of others.

Those who assume major responsibility for the way in which spouse, children, subordinates, or friends feel or behave complicate life unnecessarily and set themselves up for more problems than necessary. I am responsible for holding an interesting, quality family home evening regularly, but I am not responsible for getting children to enjoy it. I am responsible for teaching my children the gospel by precept and example, but I am not responsible for causing them to believe it or to live in compliance with its standards. I am responsible for being a reasonable, loving marriage partner, but I am not responsible for causing my wife to love me or to feel satisfied with me as a husband. I have a responsibility to visit, to care for, to instruct, and to encourage in good works the families I home teach. I am not responsible if they choose not to follow my example and advice.

It would be a serious mistake to become self-centered and to assume that what we do does not influence others. It does. And we have an obligation to make our example to the world as positive as possible. But we do not have ultimate responsibility for the behavior or feelings of others, only for our thoughts and actions with respect to our fellow men.

The Whites found out what happens when we mistakenly assume responsibility for the behavior of another individual. John White, age nineteen, had been called on a mission, and the whole family was seated on the stand to present a sacrament meeting program prior to John's departure. You could see the look of pride in his parents' faces. They did not say so directly, but one could almost see in their actions and hear in their voices that, in their minds, John's mission represented their own triumph as parents. They might not have been perfect parents, but they must have done something right because John was going on a mission.

Unfortunately, John only managed to stay three days in the Missionary Training Center when guilt forced him to admit to the mission president that he had lied during his worthiness interviews. Actually, his girl friend was already pregnant at the time of his interviews. John's parents were totally crushed. Any set of parents would be saddened by such a turn of events, but the Whites took the problem personally. They had accepted responsibility for the positive outcome, so now they were forced to accept responsibility for the negative.

Of course, in reality the Whites were not responsible for either the apparent success or the apparent failure of their son. Assuming that they had done a reasonable job of teaching the gospel and of encouraging a mission, they were successful in this respect no matter what the outcome for John. If they had not taught the gospel and had not set a good example, they were unsuccessful in regard to encouraging a mission no matter what the outcome. Why? The Whites could control their actions, but not John's. Therefore, they should evaluate the effectiveness of their performance on the basis of *their* performance, not on John's.

The same point can be made with respect to events that are beyond one's control. Suppose that Ruth is driving with reasonable care and observing traffic regulations, but a child darts out into the street and is run over and killed by her vehicle. Although Ruth will feel great sorrow over the situation and sincere sympathy for the parents of the child, she is not responsible for the child's death. It occurred because of events beyond Ruth's control. True, she theoretically might have paid more attention to the road or she might have reacted faster, but Ruth was driving as specified by law and she was driving no differently than any other average driver on the road. Sorrow would be inevitable, but it would not be necessary for Ruth to feel guilty.

Even though we may not face dramatic situations of the type Ruth experienced, we are prone to accept responsibility in countless little ways for events over which we do not have control. All of us legitimately are responsible for so many problems that we simply cannot afford the emotional energy to worry about things for which we are *not* responsible.

There Are Limits to What We Can Control

A basic theme of this chapter is that we cannot control the feelings and behavior of others; therefore, we are responsible only for *our* feelings and behavior. Even God cannot, or at least normally will not, control the actions of his children. Because of our need to be tested and to experience evil as well as good, events over which we have no control must be allowed to unfold even if they have short-term negative consequences. Ultimately God's purposes will all be fulfilled, but not by his overruling man's free agency. Parents, spouses, home teachers, or others who forget this principle of agency and try to force conformity in others are usually disappointed. Forced conformity, as we decided before this life, is really no victory at all.

Moreover, there are limits on our control when it comes to our own behavior (see chapter 1). For example, even with 100 percent effort, we do not have the capacity to do all things perfectly or to do everything at once. Reasonable responsibility, then, means assuming responsibility only for that over which we have control and remembering to respect natural limits on what we mortals can do.

It Makes Me Mad

3

Many of us unnecessarily complicate our lives by assuming responsibility for events and circumstances over which we have little or no control. On the other hand, it is also a common tendency to refuse to accept responsibility for some things for which we are, in fact, responsible. This tendency occurs primarily in connection with our emotions. Often we assume that our negative feelings are caused by circumstances and events outside of ourselves: ''He made me mad''; ''It depresses me''; ''If Jane loves me I will be happy.'' In each case we are effectively giving up control of how we feel and passing that responsibility to events or circumstances outside of ourselves, and, incidently, to circumstances beyond our control.

An emotion can be defined as a physiological response to both what we perceive *and* what we believe or think about our perceptions. The root cause of our feelings is not what happens to us, but what we think about it. Suppose that while standing in line at the bank I am bumped sharply from behind. The perception of being bumped combined with thoughts such as *What a rude jerk, no one has a right to push me like that, I won't stand for such treatment* results in my having angry feelings and perhaps giving an angry response as I turn around to confront the "attacker."

Nothing in the situation itself *causes* me to become angry. The emotion is both caused by and controlled by what I am perceiving and thinking in response to the event. As I turn around, it becomes obvious that the person responsible is blind, also apologetic. My anger dissipates immediately and is replaced by guilt as I think, *The guy couldn't help it. What a jerk I am for getting upset over such a small thing.* In this case the same event (being bumped from behind) resulted in two different sets of emotions, depending on how the event was perceived and what thoughts were associated with it. But, again, the incident itself neither caused nor controlled my emotions.

As another example, I am driving down the road and notice in the rearview mirror a patrol car approaching rapidly with red lights flashing. I perceive that I am being signaled to stop (or in other words that I've been had) which results in a panicky, uncomfortable sensation. I think, *My wife will kill me; I can't afford a ticket; It isn't fair.* As the patrol car rushes by to some other assignment the sick feeling vanishes as fast as it came. In relief I think, *What a break! Thank heaven for small favors.* Again, in this instance the emotion was controlled by my perception of the situation and by what I was telling myself in relation to it, not by the event itself.

What we perceive and what we tell ourselves are also the controlling factors in more complicated emotional responses. Let's go back to Ann, whose situation was briefly described in chapter 2. Ann had experienced a very difficult twenty-year marriage. At that point, Fred indicated that he was in love with another woman and wanted a divorce. This situation resulted in a number of very intense emotions for Ann. But it was what Ann thought about the situation and not the situation itself that controlled her emotional response. At times she would *think* of how she must have failed Fred for this to have happened. That kind of thinking caused Ann to feel guilty. At other times she became incensed when she *thought* of how unfair Fred was being and how he had no right to do this to her. And still at other times Ann became fearful as she *thought* of how lonely and economically insecure the future would be.

It is true that Ann would not have had these emotions if Fred had not decided to divorce her, but that does not mean Fred *caused* Ann to hurt, at least not directly. Ann was treated unfairly by Fred; however, Ann is the only one responsible for her emotional reaction. Unless she recognizes this fact, she will be at the mercy of the situation and of Fred's manipulation. Elder Sterling W. Sill quotes Brigham Young as saying, ''He who takes offense where none was intended is a fool — but he is a fool who takes offense whether it was intended or not'' (*The Laws of Success* [Salt Lake City: Deseret Book Co., 1977], p. 126).

In a lighter vein, but illustrating the same principle, I would not have had four doughnuts too many this morning if (1) I had not been in the kitchen, and (2) if the doughnuts had not been there. But, of course, neither my being in the kitchen nor the presence of the doughnuts caused me to eat them. That decision (unfortunately) was mine.

You Are in Control

Other people and events influence, but do not control, how we feel. If Ann is in Fred's presence when he is being negative, it will be more difficult for her to think positive, constructive thoughts. But, just the same, it will not be impossible. If she is both prepared and determined, Ann can remain relatively unruffled emotionally even during a heavy attack from Fred. On the other hand, if she is with a supportive friend, it will be easier for Ann to think right and, therefore, to be emotionally calm. Although Ann might conclude that talking with her best friend *made* her feel better, the truth is that Ann's concepts and attitudes became more positive when directed to and reinforced by her friend. Ann's thoughts were still the controlling factor.

The difficulty of accepting this theory is two-fold. First,

our emotional reactions occur with great speed; and second, we often do not consciously relate our thoughts to our emotions. But, in fact, we do a lot of things without giving direct thought to them — driving a car, tying our shoes, and washing our hands. It has been my experience in years of counseling that we also respond emotionally to many events by habit. That is, we habitually tend to think the same thoughts in given situations. In effect, our attitudes and opinions program us to feel a certain way. Given a specific event, with the appropriate cue, a program runs through our computer and an emotion emerges, all without conscious thought on our part and sometimes with such speed that we are unaware of the process.

Yet under normal circumstances we are still in control. We are the ones who program ourselves. Other people and events may influence our thinking, but they do not control our basic attitudes.

Another aspect of control is that we have the ability to change an unpleasant emotion after it has appeared. For example, many people easily become angry at being cut off by another driver on the freeway. But as they change certain underlying attitudes and assumptions (as discussed in a later example), the habit of responding in anger can be eliminated. Even before they have arrived at the point of eliminating anger, they can rid themselves of the angry response after it emerges by using appropriate self-talk. For example, they might think: *Relax, no use making myself upset; he probably isn't a rude so-and-so even though he just acted like one*. But if the emotion is allowed to play itself out and is reinforced with thoughts, such as *I won't let that ignorant so-and-so get away with it,* it becomes increasingly difficult to control angry feelings.

Important Concepts for Emotional Stability

Following the reasoning presented thus far, we can see that our attitudes and concepts about the world and about ourselves definitely influence how we feel. Our attitudes define what we think; and, in turn, what we think controls how we feel.

The combination of what we think and how we feel determines how we behave. Perhaps Elder Sterling W. Sill had this in mind when he wrote the following:

> For generations we have largely overlooked the greatest single cause of human failure and suffering: our emotions. We need far more than a sound body and a keen intellect to get us comfortably through life. We need a sound philosophy of life. (*The Laws of Success,* p. 126.)

The appropriate philosophy of life can be found in the gospel of Jesus Christ. Complementary notions also can be found in the works of Albert Ellis and Maxie Maultsby. Although these two therapists, particularly Dr. Ellis, are not religious in their orientation, several of their notions complement gospel principles which we sometimes miss in our religious study. A few of their ideas, along with some of my own, are summarized below. The reader is referred to several works[1] for more information on the philosophy of Drs. Ellis and Maultsby.

Concept 1: I can choose to feel the way I want to in any situation. This concept is a major point of the preceding discussion. We often assume that emotional control involves some magic that is beyond us. But, in fact, we *are* capable of controlling how we feel. Emotional control is a skill that can be developed by all of us. The main obstacle to doing so, however, is in assuming that control is an impossible task.

Concept 2: I can accept myself, even though I do not seem to be loved by some people. Many individuals cannot accept themselves because they feel a lack of love from a spouse, close friend, or parent. The conscious or subconscious assumption usually is *These are the people who know me best and, therefore, the people who should love me; if they don't, there must be*

[1] Albert Ellis and Robert A. Harper, *A New Guide to Rational Living* (Hollywood: Wilshire Book Co., 1977). Albert Ellis and Russell Grieger, *Handbook of Rational-Emotive Therapy* (New York: Springer, 1977). Maxie C. Maultsby, Jr., *Help Yourself to Happiness* (New York: Institute of Living, 1975).

something terribly wrong with me. In fact, if the majority of people with whom we relate do not accept us, it is probably a good clue that something is wrong in our behavior. But lack of acceptance from a *specific* person when most others seem to respect us often represents either something unhealthy in that person or in our relationship with that individual. It does not necessarily signal a general problem with our behavior.

Sometimes we are not accepted because the other person involved is incapable of feeling love for anyone. Reasons for this include fear of rejection and low self-esteem. More commonly, however, we find that others actually do love us but do not express those feelings, at least not in the way we are expecting. Then, too, feelings of acceptance may be deliberately withheld in order to hurt or manipulate us. Whatever the cause of lack of acceptance, we certainly paint ourselves into a corner if we depend on specific people to accept or love us before we can be happy.

Concept 3: The way I act does not necessarily tell me what kind of person I am. Ruth was arrested for shoplifting on two occasions and had stolen other items without being caught. In Ruth's mind (and in the minds of many others) she is a thief. In fact, Ruth is not happy about her stealing; she feels guilty about it and has made several attempts to stop it. The primary problem that leads her to compulsive shoplifting is a poor self-image. Each time she defines herself as a thief that image suffers more, and the probability of her stealing actually increases. Ruth does steal, and she will suffer negative consequences until she works through the problem. But thievery has not worked itself into her personality. She does not enjoy it, look forward to it, excuse it, or condone it.

My two-year-old is noisy, selfish, self-centered, messy, and generally not worth much if we consider only her behavior or her present contributions to the family. Yet she has tremendous value. It is not possible to determine the kind of person she is at this point because she is still developing into that person. I believe the same thing is true of adults. We are still becoming the kind of person we can be. Ultimately, yes, the kind of person we've been will determine our eternal future; but for now, it is too early to judge either ourselves or others. Very likely each of us knows someone who has made a dramatic change in his or her life, sometimes very suddenly. Unfortunately, in some cases the change is toward more negative behavior; but in other cases, people move from wickedness to righteousness.

The point is that it does no good to assume that one is either a "good" or "bad" person, based on his behavior at any given point in this life. We need to evaluate our *behavior* as being either good or bad but, at the same time, maintain a basic belief that we are good and that we have inherent value regardless of what we do. One who insists that he is a "bad" person, as opposed to a good person who sometimes does bad things, ignores the fact that he is literally the offspring of God, and he denies the scriptures which indicate his eternal worth and god-like potential.

Concept 4: Almost nothing I face in life is terrible or awful. Situations can be described as difficult, uncomfortable, hard to deal with, and unfortunate, but rarely is it accurate to label situations as terrible or awful. I can think of very few circumstances in which coping would be impossible. Take, for example, the death of a young mother in an automobile accident. She left five children under the age of eight. Some might call that awful; certainly her husband would be tempted to define the situation as a catastrophe. But actually no one's chance for happiness in life or hope of eternal exaltation was jeopardized or permanently impaired because of the accident.

Of course, if those involved assume that the event is terrible or awful and that it will limit their opportunity for happiness, that is exactly what will happen. But it does not need to happen that way. In fact, in the example given, self-pity and "awfulizing" were short-lived. The husband soon remarried, and all parties involved carried on their lives effectively.

As another example, the Saints in Jackson County, Missouri, in 1833 suffered greatly. Some two hundred homes were destroyed; the Saints suffered much abuse and loss of property, and some even lost their lives. Section 101 of the Doctrine and Covenants was given in response to the Missouri troubles; and it is important to note that the Lord said, in effect, "Don't worry about it."

> Yet I will own them, and they shall be mine in that day when I shall come to make up my jewels. (Verse 3.)
>
> And all they who have mourned shall be comforted.
>
> And all they who have given their lives for my name shall be crowned. (Verses 14-15.)

Much of section 101 talks about the beautiful conditions of the Millennium and about the justice of God. For the Saints tempted to awfulize their situation, the Lord was saying, "It really is not terrible from *my* perspective. I am in control, and all things will work for the good of those who serve me."

In short, nothing that happens to us which does not have eternal implications (including death, disease, handicaps, loss of friends, incapacitation, and economic difficulty) is awful. To tell ourselves that it is, simply reduces our ability to successfully cope with the problem. It is also true that sins need not be awful if we repent. Even grave sins can be repented of; and as they are, the promise is that it will be as if those sins had never been committed. To me, that doesn't sound awful. The real tragedy comes when we refuse to recognize our sins, consider the future hopeless, or become so discouraged with ourselves and our "awful" predicaments that we quit trying.

Concept 5: Perfection is a step-by-step process in which mistakes are necessary. The concept that perfection is a step-by-step process in which mistakes are necessary is discussed in chapter 1. An effective tool Lucifer uses with those who are striving for excellence is to encourage us to accept unrealistic standards of performance and then to get us to depreciate ourselves and others when we fall short of those standards.

As was stated in chapter 1, we should not expect to be perfect in everything. We have a tendency to generalize the Savior's statement "Be ye therefore perfect, even as your Father which is in heaven is perfect" (Matthew 5:48) to include a concern that we be flawless in every endeavor. A careful reading, however, suggests that the Lord was talking about being perfect in charity. He wasn't necessarily talking about being a perfect homemaker, a perfect business executive, or a perfect artist. His injunction (both in Matthew 5:44-48 and 3 Nephi 12:44-48) comes in the context of instruction to bless those who treat us badly and to do good to all men, in other words, to be charitable. Doctrine and Covenants 88:125 is also instructive. There we are counseled to "clothe [ourselves] with the bond of charity, as with a mantle, which is the *bond of perfectness* and peace" (italics added). It certainly becomes more difficult to be perfect in charity if we are constantly irritated by others who make it impossible for us to be perfect in wordly pursuits.

Concept 6: I am responsible only for that over which I have control. This idea also was treated in detail earlier. An allegory is used here to again emphasize the point. Suppose that I have a goal to walk with a group of people ten miles in extreme heat. As we go along, others begin casting off articles of clothing. If I felt obligated to pick up the discarded items and add them to my own load, I would soon be laboring under a very heavy weight. Because of the added load, I would begin to move slower and slower, exerting more and more energy but making less and less progress.

If I picked up too much excess baggage, there would be some danger that eventually I could not move at all under the weight. At best, I would cover the ten miles only with great exertion. As I notice that others have covered the same distance with a lighter load and that they are not even breathing hard, I may feel angry about the inequity of it all. But is it inequitable? I was the one who picked up the excess baggage, and I was the one unwilling to let it go.

So it is with life. We often take on so much excess baggage along the way that we end up breathless, tired, and discouraged because of the heavy load. If we will remember to carry only the load of our own responsibilities, those things over which we are meant to have control, our trip through life will be much less burdensome.

Concept 7: I do not need fair and equitable treatment from the world in order to be happy. There is considerable inequity in the world. It really does not seem fair that equally hard workers doing similar jobs in the same location receive different salaries, that some people are better looking or more intelligent than others, that crime pays (at least in this life), that conditions from culture to culture or from neighborhood to neighborhood vary so much, that some people have physical or emotional handicaps and others do not, and that some people have unstable environments during infancy. Some people make problems for themselves when (1) they assume that things ought to be fair, and (2) they condemn God, others, or themselves for the inequities that affect them.

But, in fact, inequity does and will exist, and the only reasonable thing to do is to accept that fact and not fight it, even though we should try to correct what specific inequities we can. We can have faith that justice and equity will triumph in the end. While life may not be fair to everyone, we can be assured that eternity will be. We know that crime pays only on this side of the veil, and that there will be an accounting and a price to pay for misdeeds even if the price is not exacted here. We also know that no one will be able to quarrel with God's fairness at the final accounting.

Fortunately, inequity need not rob us of happiness here. It is just as possible for the less good-looking to find happiness in life as it is for the handsome, and as easy for the poor as for the rich (sometimes easier). The difficulty comes when individuals assume that they cannot be happy because of some problem they face. Viktor Frankl tells us that there were victims in concentration camps who found happiness, and we know of others who have found happiness even when crippled with debilitating and incurable disease.[2] As suggested earlier, events and cir-

---

[2]Viktor Frankl, *Man's Search for Meaning* (Boston: Beacon Press, 1962).

cumstances don't seem to be as important as our attitude about those events.

Concept 8: I can be happier in the long run by facing life's difficulties head-on. Many of the choices we make in life constitute a decision between short-term and long-term comfort. Those who consistently opt for short-term comfort suffer more in the long run. A shy individual, for example, avoids social contact because such contact is uncomfortable for him. By not facing the short-term discomfort, the individual cuts himself off from people and leads a lonely and exceptionally uncomfortable life in the long run. Someone in need of losing weight may decide to eat at will in order to be more comfortable at the moment; of course, in the long run that person is very uncomfortable because of the impact extra weight has on self-esteem, social relations, and general health.

This same notion has obvious implications for the next life. Those who have firmly implanted in their minds the concept that it is better to be uncomfortable at the moment than in the long run are much more likely to reach their celestial goals.

Developing the Skill of Emotional Control

As suggested earlier, developing emotional control is really a two-stage process. The first stage involves being certain that our assumptions about life are reasonable and rational. Since much of our emotional response is habitual and automatically controlled by our philosophies of life, we need to be wholly converted to the concepts outlined above and described throughout this book. The second stage involves practice. We must learn to get in touch with what we are thinking, to understand what causes us to feel and think a certain way, and then to learn how to modify those thoughts. One procedure for doing so is described below.

When we are having feelings we do not want (especially soon after those feelings have emerged), we must first ask ourselves what we were thinking or doing that caused us to feel that way. Next, we need to write down what comes to mind.

The process will not have much value if it is completed in one's head. *The thoughts must be written down.* Following this, we should ask ourselves why those ideas bother us, and then write down additional thoughts that come to mind. This results in a list of several concepts which very likely are the ones causing us emotional upset. At that point we need to assess how correct each of these thoughts is and to modify those concepts which contradict our emotional goal. Finally, it is important that we review intensely the new way of thinking generated by this process.

In narrative form this approach probably sounds laborious and much more trouble than it is worth. Actually, it takes only a few minutes and saves much time and energy that would otherwise be wasted in unpleasant feelings, such as anger or depression. The procedure is described next in terms of two real-life examples.

Situation 1. Jason is late for supper again. He is an hour overdue, and he has not called. He says that pressures at work cause him to be late and that he thinks about calling but then gets involved in emergencies. Terri has complained about Jason's lack of thoughtfulness. When she does, he apologizes — but it seems to happen again anyway. On this particular occasion Terri is angry. She is also feeling jealousy and fear. It is an uncomfortable situation for Terri, and her mood is beginning to influence the children. Getting out her pencil and paper, she asks herself what she must be thinking that is causing her to feel this way. (Note: If she assumed that Jason was the cause, she would have no incentive to do something about her own anger other than to yell at him.)

Step 1: What am I thinking that is causing me to feel this way?

a. Jason must not love me, or he would be more sensitive to my needs.
b. He is probably goofing off; he couldn't be that busy.
c. Maybe he has a girl friend.

d. It's not fair; I've gone to a lot of trouble to fix his dinner.

Step 2: Why do these thoughts bother me?

e. I must have Jason's love, or I can't be happy.
f. Jason has an exciting life, and I have to take care of kids all day.
g. I would kill Jason (or myself) if I found out he had a girl friend; I couldn't stand it.
h. I need respect, and I don't get it from Jason.

Step 3: How shall I evaluate how rational each thought is on the combined list (from Steps 1 and 2)? (Note: In order for a thought to be rational, it must be both true *and* supportive of one's emotional goal.)

a. Jason must not love me, or he would be more sensitive to my needs. *Not rational* because: Jason does a lot of things to demonstrate his love. Insensitive behavior does not necessarily mean no love. I sometimes don't do what he wants (he says that is being insensitive), even though I love him. The thought makes me feel terrible.
b. He is probably goofing off. He couldn't be that busy. *Not rational* because:
I don't know how busy he is. Why assume anything? The end of the day is probably his busiest. I don't care as much about how busy he is as I do about how busy I am. The thought makes me feel jealous and angry.
c. Maybe he has a girl friend. *Not rational* because:
His being late is not good evidence. I have no other reason to suspect Jason. No use worrying about something before it happens. The thought makes me feel angry and afraid.

d. It's not fair. I have gone to a lot of trouble. *True, but not rational* because:
It is unfair, but primarily Jason is the one missing out. The kids and I can enjoy the meal anyway. I did not have to go to the trouble I did; I chose to. The thought makes me angry.

e. I must have Jason's love or I can't be happy. *Not rational* because:
I want Jason's love, but I do not need it to survive. Without his love I will not die or lose a chance for exaltation. I, not Jason, am in charge of how I feel. The thought is very frustrating.

f. Jason has an exciting life, and I have to take care of kids all day. *Not rational* because:
I don't know how exciting his life is; he actually has a lot of pressure. I can get baby-sitters and take more breaks than I do. I can make my life more exciting. The thought makes me angry.

g. I would kill Jason or myself if I found out he had a girl friend. I couldn't stand it. *Not rational* because:
Obviously I could stand it. I would not like it, but I could stand it. I am not going to kill anybody. The thought makes me feel terrible.

h. I need respect, and I don't get it from Jason. *Not rational* because:
I don't get respect when it comes to this issue, but in other ways I do. I have the respect of myself and of many people. I want, but I do not need, Jason's respect. The thought hurts me a lot.

Step 4: How shall I modify the thoughts in order to make them more rational (i.e., think thoughts which more accurately describe the situation and which help me feel less negative emotion)?

1. Jason is insensitive in this respect, but he does love me.
2. No use making myself upset about our different life-styles.
3. I can make my own life more stimulating and exciting.
4. I will not jump to the conclusion that Jason has a girl friend; that assumption will not help either of us.
5. Jason is the one who is missing out if he isn't home on time.
6. I refuse to worry about it.
7. Jason very likely does respect me; but whether he does or not, the important thing is that I respect myself. Respecting myself will be hard if I get uptight over this thing.

Step 5: I will review the new thinking intensely.

At this point Terri committed the list of new thoughts to memory and reviewed them in her mind repeatedly as she went about her routine over the next hour. *Result:* Terri remained somewhat disturbed, but she moderated her emotions dramatically. She did not incite a riot when Jason arrived home, although she did express her displeasure. She also made plans to get involved in racquetball weekly and to have one evening out a week for herself.

Situation 2. It was pointed out earlier that some people program themselves to react angrily when they are cut off by a careless driver in traffic. Ed had such an experience on the way to work. The anger he felt during and after the incident was painful in itself, but he was more uncomfortable and embarrassed over the childish way he had acted (almost causing an accident) in response to his angry feeling. Now at work, Ed took out a paper and pencil and spent five to ten minutes evaluating his feelings.

Step 1: What was I thinking that caused me to feel that way?

a. The guy is a rude, careless jerk.
b. This is my lane.
c. He almost killed me.
d. I can't let him get away with it.

Step 2: Why did those thoughts bother me?

e. I cannot tolerate rude, careless jerks.
f. No one has a right to take away my rights or possessions.
g. I don't want to die.
h. My integrity as a person has been violated.

Step 3: How shall I evaluate how rational each thought is?

a. The guy is a rude, careless jerk. *Not rational* because:
I don't even know the person. Smart, considerate people do dumb, inconsiderate things occasionally. I have done the same thing to others, and I am no jerk. The thought makes me angry.

b. This is my lane. *Not rational* because:
It is a public highway. I do not see my name anywhere on the road. The thought makes me angry.

c. He almost killed me. *Not rational* because:
It was not really that close a call. I might have been killed by an accident, but the guy was not aiming at me. My childish reaction was more dangerous than the initial incident. The thought makes me angry.

d. I can't let him get away with it. *Not rational* because:
He received nothing to get away with. He probably felt dumb about it himself. I only hurt myself by making a big issue out of it, and I almost caused an accident myself. The thought makes me angry.

e. I can't tolerate rude, careless jerks. *Not rational* because:
Obviously, I can tolerate most anything if I choose to. I would not have to relate to this guy in the future unless by making a big deal out of it I get into a confrontation. I can tolerate myself, yet I acted rude and careless in response to my anger. The thought makes me angry.

f. No one has a right to take away my rights or possessions. *True, but not rational* because:
I become a double victim by getting upset about a loss. (I am victimized first by the loss and second by an emotional reaction to it.) This person did not really take anything from me. The thought makes me angry.

g. I don't want to die. *True, but not rational* because:
No use worrying about something that did not happen. It really was not that close a call. The thought makes me worry.

h. My integrity as a person has been violated. *Not rational* because:
No one but me can violate my integrity as a person. It was an accident, not an intentional insult. The thought makes me angry.

Step 4: How shall I modify the thoughts to make them more rational?

1. People who do stupid, inconsiderate things

on the road are not necessarily stupid, inconsiderate people.

2. Insensitive acts are a part of life; I only complicate things unnecessarily if I get uptight about them.
3. Making a big deal or trying to get even with the guy only victimizes me further.
4. It isn't that big a deal anyway.
5. I do not have to get uptight.

Step 5: I will review the new thinking intensely.
Ed copied the new thoughts on a three-by-five card and placed the card on his dashboard. He committed the thoughts to memory and repeated them out loud several times while driving to and from work for a week. *Result:* Ed was much less inclined to be uptight during his daily commute. He found himself slipping again after a few weeks, but by taking out the card and reminding himself of the correct thinking on the point, he quickly solved the problem again.

Emotional Control Is a Reasonable Goal

A major focus of this chapter has been to emphasize that emotional control is a reasonable goal. We can learn to control how we feel by learning to control what we think. The reader is given some further pointers in chapter 9 on how to develop the skill of emotional control. Suppose, as a final thought, that God had not developed that skill. It is frightening to think of an omnipotent being who is not in control of his emotions and, therefore, who is in the habit of using his unlimited power in capricious and immature ways. It would be impossible to respect such a being or to comfortably and voluntarily follow him. Thinking about it in that way, we recognize that it is impossible for us to become joint-heirs with Christ and to share in the power he has without first having developed complete self-mastery.

Guilt and the "I Have To's" 4

Guilt can be a useful clue in reminding us that our present conduct is inappropriate and that it will result in damage if persisted in over the long run. Guilt can be thought of as the moral equivalent of pain. If the body is functioning properly, putting a hand on a hot stove hurts. The pain is an effective warning that inevitable tissue damage will result if one's hand is not removed from the stove. Guilt, likewise, is an uncomfortable condition that can signal the need to remove oneself from a form of conduct that will inevitably lead to emotional or spiritual damage.

The problem is that we sometimes feel guilty when there is no need to, which essentially is the subject of chapter 1. We create a false sense of error within ourselves and then waste energy fighting what really isn't a problem at all. For example, we assume that there is something wrong with us if we are not doing everything we do flawlessly. Diverting our energies down the wrong channels often allows legitimate weaknesses in our behavior to go unresolved. Another problem with guilt is that we let it become all-consuming. The signal, that which was designed to warn us of trouble, becomes the trouble. It is not uncommon, for example, for an individual to foster feelings of guilt long after he has repented of the sin. Some individuals also let guilt develop to the point that they actually immobilize themselves and give away the power within to repent.

The Problem of Self-blame

Instances in which guilt is overdone or in which a person feels excessive guilt usually involve self-blame or self-condemnation. Albert Ellis wrote:

> We can designate the essence of emotional disturbance in a single word: blaming — or damning. If you would stop, really stop, damning yourself, others, or unkind fate, you would find it virtually impossible to feel emotionally upset about anything. And you can probably omit "virtually" from the preceding sentence. (*A New Guide to Rational Living,* p. 113.)

This point rings true. Self-blame is at the heart of most emotional disturbance. But from a religious perspective, anesthetizing guilt would remove an important and necessary inner "traffic light." Up to a point, self-blame is useful. At least it can help us to accept responsibility for our misconduct. But when we accept responsibility, emotional disturbance is usually inevitable. Alma, for example, describes the intense guilt he felt because of past sins:

> But I was racked with eternal torment, for my soul was harrowed up to the greatest degree and racked with all my sins.
>
> Yea, I did remember all my sins and iniquities, for which I was tormented with the pain of hell; yea, I saw that I had rebelled against my God, and that I had not kept his holy commandments.
>
> Yea, and I had murdered many of his children, or rather led them away unto destruction; yea, and in fine so great had been my iniquities, that the very thought of coming into the presence of my God did rack my soul with inexpressible horror.

> Oh, thought I, that I could be banished and become extinct both soul and body, that I might not be brought to stand in the presence of my God, to be judged of my deeds. (Alma 36:12-15.)

This pain was useful to Alma, who then found motivation to seek Christ and a forgiveness of sins. Once that was accomplished, guilt had served its purpose and Alma was able to accept his Savior and to forgive himself.

> Now, as my mind caught hold upon this thought, I cried within my heart: O Jesus, thou Son of God, have mercy on me, who am in the gall of bitterness, and am encircled about by the everlasting chains of death.
>
> And now, behold, when I thought this, I could remember my pains no more; yea, I was harrowed up by the memory of my sins no more.
>
> And oh, what joy, and what marvelous light I did behold; yea, my soul was filled with joy as exceeding as was my pain! (Alma 36:18-20.)

After accepting Christ, Alma did not blame others for the wrong he had done. He did not blame God. Neither, apparently, did he blame himself. Alma's forgiving himself required an understanding that mortals will make mistakes (concept 5 in chapter 3) and that good people do bad things occasionally (concept 3, chapter 3). So as he would fully obey the Lord's commandments after his conversion, he no longer needed to worry about the consequences of his sins, because he had faith in Jesus Christ, and he knew that the demands of justice were satisfied by his Savior.

Overcoming self-blame. Doris was excommunicated from the Church for adultery, actually for a series of adulterous encounters. To her credit, she continued to attend Church and worked her way back to full membership. Guilt was useful to Doris; without it she would not have been motivated to confront her problem. Without any feelings of guilt, she would have innocently and blissfully gone on until the final day of accounting, at which time she would have been told that her eternal potential was now limited. If Doris had felt some guilt because of her behavior, but not painful guilt, she likely would have gone on feeling uncomfortable and suffering to some extent — but not feeling uncomfortable enough to get rid of the problem once and for all.

Even though the overall influence of guilt was good, at times she let her guilt feelings get out of hand, almost to the point of giving up altogether. Sometimes Doris would let herself assume that she was a weak, evil person in whom God could have little interest or respect. She got into the business of condemning herself rather than the sin. Once this happened, a sense of hopelessness overpowered her, taking with it the incentive to continue repenting. Also at this time Doris got into the habit of blaming others, which, incidentally, almost always follows blaming oneself. Doris criticized the Church for treating her harshly, her bishop for not being more helpful, her family for neglecting her, her friends for not understanding, and God for letting it all happen. Guilt was helpful initially, but blame was absolutely counterproductive.

Actually, Doris had some legitimate complaints. Her bishop was overloaded, and he could have been more helpful. Her family members had their own problems which led them at times to neglect Doris's feelings. Even God apparently was not always there. At times he was shut out by Doris's attitude; at other times, perhaps, in his wisdom, he allowed Doris to resolve issues on her own. The point is that it did Doris no good to blame herself or others. Inequities exist in life, but they do not have to seriously disturb us unless we let them.

But as Doris changed her thinking, her attitude about herself improved and her tendency (need) to blame others disappeared. Doris had to remind herself hourly during the initial climb out of depression that she was a worthwhile, capable individual, deserving of both her own and God's respect. She had committed sin, but that did not make her an evil, corruptible person. Doris learned that all behavior can be changed and that we always have the option to forsake error.

Doris told herself that everyone makes mistakes, many of them sins to be feared. But, feared or not, they are to be learned from. This kind of self-talk (the dialogue we have with ourselves) helped Doris considerably.

Doris also derived strength by emphasizing the relationship she had with the Lord. She tried a form of emotive imagery (chapter 9) in which she relaxed completely and tried to picture the Savior in several scenes. One involved the woman taken in adultery (see John 8:3-11). Doris tried to picture Jesus's sensitive response and the emotional relief of the young woman as she went her way. Another picture involved the Savior's appearance to the Nephites and the sincere, loving relationship he had with those people. Doris then imagined that she had completed the repentance process and that she was being received by the Lord. She pictured the peace and joy that would be hers in that situation.

Doris also reviewed the scriptures for every instruction she could find relative to atonement, forgiveness, charity, and love. This scripture review led Doris to a witness that she was accepted by the Lord, that her sins were forgiven, and that she still had every opportunity for a celestial outcome. What a sense of relief she felt as that burden was lifted!

Once her self-talk was appropriate and once Doris had rekindled her faith in Christ and the Atonement, she, like Alma, was able to stop blaming herself and others. But Lucifer was not finished with Doris yet. Doris went to her bishop and asked for rebaptism. After prayer and deliberation, the bishop indicated that he felt it necessary for Doris to wait another six months before considering rebaptism. Just as Lucifer hoped, Doris was totally crushed. All of the doubts she had before about her self-worth flooded back, along with the inevitable blaming of self and others that are companions to such doubts.

What Doris overlooked was the fact that forgiveness by the Lord and the way the ecclesiastical authority handles the person's return to full fellowship will not necessarily be on the same time schedule. Contrary to concept 4 in chapter 3, she was assuming that not being baptized immediately was a terrible, awful thing and that she couldn't possibly be happy unless this event took place immediately. Although she was not pleased about it, the necessity of waiting to be baptized did not have to make her unhappy in general, and it had no direct impact whatsoever on her eternal future. The only thing that did matter in the long run was how she handled this sudden disappointment.

Doris again found it necessary to watch her self-talk carefully and to again emphasize her relationship with Christ. But she did this successfully and continued faithful and, by so doing, brought a growing peace and happiness into her life.

Here is another example to illustrate the price we pay for blaming: a man with a responsible Church leadership position was also an independent businessman who made his living in real estate. A couple, also members of the Church, decided to invest in a condominium project recommended by this man. They arranged for a second mortgage on their home to provide the needed cash. Unfortunately, the project was not successful, and the couple lost most of their money. They were not people of means, and the situation seriously hurt them financially.

In this case there may have been error on both sides. The Church leader perhaps was overly optimistic about the project and should not have marketed it as strongly as he did to people who could ill afford the loss. On the other hand, the couple involved were probably after a get-rich-quick opportunity and should have investigated thoroughly before investing in the project, especially given their financial circumstances.

As so often happens in situations of this nature, the couple became very bitter. Their first inclination was to blame themselves — the husband for making the decision, and the wife for letting it be made. But self-blame was too uncomfortable, and they soon gave that up and began to blame one another instead. "You idiot, why were you so stupid?" said the wife to her husband. "If you weren't so money-hungry, I would not have been pushed into investing," said the husband to his wife.

When blaming one another became too uncomfortable,

they began to blame the businessman who had encouraged them to invest. All told, they wasted much energy and time in hating this person and in trying to get even for the trouble they assumed he had caused them. To make matters worse, the couple quit attending church. They even began to blame the Church for not disfellowshipping or excommunicating the Church leader in question.

Blaming makes us double victims. The above example is a classic case of how we can easily become double victims, which always happens when we decide to cast blame on ourselves, on others, or on an organization. The couple in the case cited are out a great deal of money, which makes life more difficult than it would be otherwise. But there is nothing they can do about that now. To make themselves upset does not help the situation but compounds it. As a result of the feelings they have chosen to have, they are not only out the money but now they are also unhappy and bitter. (They don't have to be happy about losing the money, but they should not make themselves generally unhappy because of the loss.)

By cutting themselves off from the Church, they have become triple victims. But, again, the incident did not cause them to remove themselves from the Church; they chose not to attend. In making a poor financial decision, they cannot avoid the financial consequences of that decision. In other words, they can do nothing about being victims should the project fail. But there is no need to become double or triple victims. At any time they can give up the blaming and return to the Church.

In order to free themselves from their uncomfortable situation, this couple would first have to change their self-talk. (Having read this far, you may wish to guess what these people must be thinking that makes them miserable.) Listen to some of their thoughts.

1. This is a terrible, awful situation.
2. This is unfair, and I cannot tolerate such injustice.
3. I will not rest until justice is done.

Filmstrips P. Behnke

34. Turn The hearts of
The Children (Genealogy) 32:00 min.

35. This is The Right Place
(Brigham Young) 13: min.

4. I will not go to Church knowing that people like him are accepted there.
5. If the Church were true, the bishop would have been inspired to see it my way.
6. He is a lousy, no-good cheat and a liar.
7. I was stupid for getting involved. Stupid! Stupid! Stupid!
8. I will suffer for the rest of my life because of this.

Imagine coming to the above conclusions and constantly repeating those notions! Doing so would soon cause a person to feel very angry and unhappy. No amount of a grin-and-bear-it philosophy would help for long if a person were converted to ideas such as those above. The following would be a much more correct and productive set of conclusions:

1. I don't like having made a mistake, but it is not the end of the world. Things that really matter — happiness, relationships, family, Church — do not have to be affected.
2. It may be unfair, but who said things have to be fair in this life?
3. I refuse to be a double victim by getting upset and by letting this influence my Church participation.
4. It was stupid to get involved, but I am not stupid. It would be more stupid to go on worrying about something I can't change.
5. I do not have to suffer over this any longer than it takes me to give it up.

If conclusions like these were reached and constantly repeated, although the couple would still regret having made the investment, they would be much less emotional about it. They would not be compounding the mistake with unproductive thoughts.

Could this be why the Lord counseled us to forgive others, including those who have done us wrong? The Lord said that failing to forgive is a greater sin than the sin of the one we have not forgiven (see D&C 64:9). Failing to forgive, then, can lead to far more suffering than is caused by the original sin. As illustrated here, the couple suffered financially; but that was not nearly as devastating as the emotional and spiritual damage they did to themselves by choosing not to forgive.

Force Words and Blame

It *should* be apparent to the reader by now that what we think in general as well as the specific conscious and subconscious dialogues we have with ourselves are powerful determinants of how we feel and behave. Now, look back at the preceding sentence and notice the word *should*. *Should* is a forceful word that works its way into countless dialogues we have with ourselves and others. Whenever it appears, it sets up a condition in which blame and/or guilt is possible. Actually, the word *should* in this case is misused. No force of logic or moral imperative demands that you have the point by now; it is simply my hope that it is both clear and understood.

Must is an even stronger word, and it would be even less appropriate in the above example. Other power words include *ought, need, can't, never,* and *always*. When such words are used, they create an intensity about the situation which traps us or locks us into feeling anxious if certain other things do not happen. This is especially true when the one using the force or power word is a loved one or a highly respected person, or when we are using such words on ourselves. Sometimes these expressions are appropriate, but more often than not they overstate the situation. Given below are several examples of the misuse of force or power words.

"I must get this project completed by 5:00 P.M."

Usually the truth is that it would be ideal to get the project completed by a certain time, but it is rarely imperative. No one dies if it is not done. No one is seriously hurt by our failure to complete the assignment, and certainly it is no sin if it is not completed. Under normal circumstances, if there was a death in the family or a sudden medical emergency that precluded your finishing the task, no one would really care overmuch. Someone else would do it, or you would do it later; but no one would seriously suffer if the project was not completed by 5:00 P.M.

This does not mean that it is inappropriate to try to complete projects by deadlines (see chapter 6 on procrastination), but it does mean that we should watch the language we use in describing the situation. Someone racing against the clock and putting tremendous pressure on himself to complete an assignment usually makes more mistakes than normal, and often he is irritable and negative with others as a result. Enormous amounts of emotional energy are expended if life is one continuous series of crises involving the "need" to do several things at once.

"I need Sharon's love."

Using the word *need* or, more appropriately, concluding that a need exists locks one into feeling terrible if the "need" is not satisfied. Many individuals have convinced themselves that they cannot live without another's love, and so they have committed suicide. No one needs to die because he feels unloved by another. We all have the need to be loved, meaning that we suffer if there is *no one* who cares about us or whom we care about. But none of us is dependent on receiving love from any particular person. Even if our mortal fathers are unloving, all of us have a loving Eternal Father; and all of us can have meaningful relationships with others, even if it seems impossible to get close to one particular person.

Obviously, people can suffer greatly when they think they need to do something or need to get something and they don't get or do it. But the suffering is usually created by the individual's definition of need rather than by the actual circumstance. Nothing in the situation mandates that someone suffer greatly if he gets passed over for promotion ("I need this chance"); or if he is rejected in romance ("I need Sharon's love"); or if he fails to be accepted into graduate school ("I need an advanced degree"); or if he makes a mistake ("I need to be perfect"). Almost invariably we can redefine situations so that we can live comfortably without the "need."

Even without redefining the situation, our "needs" can disappear over time. A person can be almost consumed with the need for a new car, but several months later not feel the need at all and be grateful he was not able to buy when he "needed" to. Another can be obsessed with the need to have a particular marriage partner, only to be grateful later that the engagement did not work out.

"I cannot tolerate Hank's criticizing me."

Can't is another powerful word that, when used and believed, traps us into feeling and behaving in certain ways. As with all force words, *can't* is appropriate at times. I can't sing with the Metropolitan Opera (for at least one obvious reason known to those who have heard me sing). I can't control the emotions and feelings of others. I can't be a physician without going to medical school. I can't be a concert pianist without some level of natural ability and years of sacrificing other things. I can't serve God and Satan at the same time.

On the other hand, in many other areas *can't* is misused. Obviously Janet *can* tolerate Hank's criticizing her if she chooses to. Most people who tell themselves they can't tolerate something from a spouse have already tolerated it for years. If someone bet Janet five thousand dollars that she could tolerate Hank's criticism for a week, she could do it. All week long Janet would be telling herself: *It is not worth getting upset about. Hank doesn't know what he is talking about anyway. I am not going to blow my five thousand dollar reward by letting Hank get to me.* Of course, Hank has no business criticizing Janet, and Janet is not obligated to sit and listen to a barrage of criticism. But if Janet tells herself that she can't take it, she is forced to feel bad and very likely to become negative and critical herself. At that point Hank has "won" in the sense that he has something legitimate to complain about in Janet's behavior.

"You always act that way."

"You always do this" or "you never do that" are common expressions in intimate relationships, but usually they are not accurate. A wife who complained that her husband never helped around the house was asked to record (unknown to her husband) what he did to help at home over a one-week period. Even with selective perception, she identified that he completed several chores and had many positive interactions with the family during the week. The husband certainly was not doing everything she wanted him to (on purpose, in most cases), but he was making a positive contribution. The wife's use of an absolute expression was not only incorrect, but also it had two direct negative outcomes: (1) it was countermotivating to the husband, who felt his efforts were not recognized, and (2) it trapped the wife into feeling more negative toward her husband and more hopeless in her situation than was necessary.

It becomes even more devastating when we use these absolutes on ourselves: "I always make mistakes" or "I never do anything right." Such conclusions trap us and cause us unnecessary discomfort and loss of self-esteem. Most people when asked about use of such absolutes will admit that the words don't really apply. "Well, I guess I don't *always* make mistakes, it just seems like it." Of course it seems like it, because that's what the person is constantly telling himself! It is actually a self-fulfilling prophecy. What we tell ourselves is a large factor in how we feel, even if we don't believe down deep what we are saying.

Misperception and unnecessary anxiety result when we tell ourselves that we *must, need, should, always,* and *never* in situations that do not require the urgency suggested by these expressions. Usually we are better off using *would like to, hope to, can, may, usually,* or *sometimes*. Referring to the concept of quasi-stationary equilibrium (chapter 1), often we feel that we *must* put pressure on ourselves in order to produce. Actually, removing obstacles to production along with establishing a more relaxed perspective, generally is a more effective way of improving our performance over the long run.

Who Likes to Be Forced?

One of the obstacles to a productive life often is a general rebellion against force. Hank, in an earlier example, was not as productive at home as he might have been simply because he was rebelling against pressure exerted by his wife. Parental pressure and force are often contributing factors in a child's unwillingness to perform up to capability at school. Many women find it very difficult to enjoy or to want to make love to their husbands in situations in which they feel pressured or forced to conform to their husbands' wishes. Obligation breeds guilt, anger, and dependency; while choice leads to love, peace, and independence. Force words, whether in terms of *you must* or *I must,* take the emphasis off choice and put it on compulsion. For that reason alone, we are better off by limiting such force words in our vocabulary.

Try an awareness exercise. Simply try to recognize the number of times you use power words in your thinking and in your conversations with others. Since much of your thinking is habitual and therefore below the awareness level, you may need to look for clues. If you are feeling pressured to perform a task, or if you are generally anxious, ask yourself what you are thinking that is causing the tension. Force words will often be there. You also might enlist the help of those close to you, asking them to point out when you use force words in conversations. Becoming aware is the first step in reducing the use of such words. As you will find, reducing the use of power language will decrease tension and anxiety without limiting performance. As a matter of fact, your performance probably will improve.

Feeling Guilty About Feeling Guilty

Once people find out that they can be in control of their emotions, they are tempted to assume that they *must* be in control at all times. (Note again the use of force or power language here.) Bill is one who fell into this trap.

Bill had a temper problem which had persisted over a number of years. He had difficulty in gaining control because he assumed that other people or events made him angry. After having had brief psychotherapy he became convinced that his thoughts and general concept system were really the culprits and that he could have complete control over his emotions if he chose to. Bill began to make exceptional progress in overcoming his problem.

After a few weeks of remarkable improvement Bill let himself again become involved in negative and irrational thinking, which caused him again to lose his temper. When that happened, Bill had one of his most severe depressive episodes ever because he suddenly concluded: *Even this doesn't work. I am no good, and there is nothing I can do about it. All my work and effort over the last few weeks was for nothing. I am as big a louse as I ever was. I will never get any better.* Bill was feeling guilty about losing his temper, as he usually did, but that guilt was compounded significantly by his new understanding that he didn't have to lose his cool.

Bill forgot the fact that emotional control is a skill that one develops over time. Mistakes, time, and, above all, continued practice are absolutely necessary when developing this skill. Making a mistake and falling into an old error did not mean that Bill had to start all over again. The progress he had made and the new understanding he had gained were his to keep unless he discredited them or gave them away. Bill's problem, in part, was that he perceived his struggle to be similar to climbing a ladder. When he slipped and fell, he was at the bottom again and had to begin to climb all over. It is more correct to view the effort as being similar to walking along a railroad tie. Sometimes we slip off and must get back on, but we don't have to go back to the point from which we originally started.

A word also should be said about feeling bad in general. Mortals are supposed to feel bad at times. Remember Lehi's point, that in order to experience joy one must also experience sorrow (see 2 Nephi 2:22-23). Everyone can expect ups and downs — periods when they feel good, and times when they don't. Sorrow is a part of living. A reasonable goal, however, is to minimize down times, to control them, and to use them constructively. Down times certainly obstruct happiness when they control us; and certainly they will control us if we feel guilty about feeling guilty.

Use Guilt, But Don't Be Used By It

As stated at the outset of this chapter, guilt serves as an inner "traffic light," and when used properly it is a valuable asset. But we can and sometimes do get the wrong signal. That does not mean that we should tear down the traffic signs, but it does suggest that we should be more discriminating in our interpretation of guilt feelings.

Sometimes we hear the concept that if we feel guilty about something, it must be wrong. It is hoped that the discussion in this chapter illustrates the fact that we can feel guilty even when there is no need to. For example, it does not help to feel guilty about feeling guilty (as discussed in the previous section) or to feel guilty even after effectively repenting, or to feel guilty when we have done no wrong. Contrary to its basic mission, guilt under these conditions weakens our ability to serve God and increases our susceptibility to temptation.

5 Reducing Problems by Reducing Stress

This chapter emphasizes what essentially is a major theme of the book. Application of the principles here discussed will result in less anxiety and less stress, and will contribute to a much more problem-free life. As an added bonus, reduced stress actually increases rather than decreases personal productivity. This is true for purely psychological reasons; but in addition, stress also has a large impact on physical health. So how we feel also plays a large role in how productive we are.

In terms of impact on health, some physicians say that stress reactions account for about 80 percent of the problems they see. In some cases stress alone causes the problems; while in others, stress is a significant factor in the ailments. This can be true with respect to problems in virtually any body organ or function, and it can be true even if a person does not feel that he is under stress.

Many of the people I see have so accommodated to stress that they generally are not aware of it. ''I feel fine,'' they maintain (often through clenched teeth), although tension is obvious in their demeanor and in their general life situation.

Even if they are not aware of it, stress is taking its toll on their bodies; and if it has not done so already, it will lead to headaches, stomach problems, or other physical complaints. Emotional symptoms too are almost invariably a part of high stress. Reactions to emotional stress range from full-blown anxiety attacks, involving difficulty in breathing and other apparent life-threatening reactions, to general irritability, lack of humor, inability to enjoy life, and inability to relax. The latter symptoms, again, may go unrecognized by the patient, but usually they are obvious to close associates.

Simple Stress Monitoring

Even though we might have accommodated to stress, normally we can recognize its presence if we monitor a few body signals. One of the easiest procedures for doing so is simply to ask ourselves how tense we are at the moment and then to rate the stress level on a hypothetical scale from one to ten (one being very relaxed, ten being very uptight). Consider whether or not your muscles are loose and relaxed. Is your body tense? Are you able to concentrate on the task at hand? Is your mind free of compulsive thoughts? Do you feel a sense of panic or pressure? Don't worry about being exact in rating the stress level; just pick a number between one and ten that seems to represent how tense you are at the moment.

Often, all that is needed in order to relax is to become aware of the tension. If you become aware that your shoulder muscles are constricted, they will almost automatically relax. If you decide that your stress level is nine or ten, it will almost automatically go down a degree or two. Letting relaxation occur automatically with awareness is ideal. Ironically, one of the best ways to create stress is to become intense about relaxing. When it comes to stress reduction, the harder you try, the more difficult it is.

Fred found himself becoming extremely tense during his daily commute. His knuckles would tighten around the steering wheel; the muscles of his neck and shoulders would tighten, as would the muscles in his forehead and around his eyes. His thoughts were preoccupied with problems in his life and/or with "what a rotten world it is." The result of this commute stress was irritability both at work and at home and a loss of enthusiasm for life.

Fred decided to monitor his stress level as suggested above. He found that at first he was usually in the eight to ten range on his stress scale; but by becoming aware of the tension level each day, he found himself relaxing and moving lower on his stress scale. By monitoring his stress problem, Fred concluded that tension was the highest on days when he was late leaving for work or home and on days when he had pressing business waiting for him on either end of his commute.

Fred therefore made a decision to leave a few minutes earlier, and he also decided to limit his worry time. He allowed himself to review his daily plan and to think about problems during the first fifteen minutes of his ride. The last fifteen minutes, however, he reserved for listening to music and daydreaming. His goal during that last fifteen minutes was to let his mind totally relax from negative or pressing issues. As a result Fred was much more relaxed both on arriving at work and on arriving home. The reduced stress also made decision-making more effective, which more than compensated for the fifteen minutes spent in mental relaxation to and from work.

Stress Cataloging

Fred was sufficiently satisfied with the results of the simple stress reduction program that he decided to do a more complete assessment of his levels of stress and of the sources of stress in his life. The three basic procedures he followed took a fair amount of time and effort in the short run, but they paid off handsomely in reduced stress over the long term. Encouraged by Fred's success, his wife, Ann, followed the same procedures. Ann's experience follows.

Procedure A: Monitor stress daily for two weeks

Ann secreted a pencil and paper in a place where she could record thoughts and feelings that she did not necessarily want to share with the family. She then put a red three-by-five card in her checkbook, one behind her toothbrush in the medicine chest, and one in the closet containing her cleaning supplies and tennis racquet. Each time during the day that she came across a three-by-five card, Ann recorded information under the headings listed below.

Day ____________________

Time	*Stress Level*	*Activities*	*Thoughts*

Under *Stress Level,* Ann recorded a number between one and ten that seemed to represent the level of tension she felt at the moment. Under *Activities,* she noted her prominent activities since the last recording. Ann also noted in the *Thoughts* category some of the main things she had been thinking about since the last entry. Over a two-week period, Ann made several recordings. Some are excerpted here.

Wednesday

Time	*Stress Level*	*Activities*	*Thoughts*
8:10 A.M.	9	scripture reading breakfast kids, Fred off	no time to myself won't do well on Relief Society lesson Sunday impossible to get kids to do chores
1:30 P.M.	3	prepared meal for sick neighbor	kids home soon no time for me
3:00 P.M.	6	house cleaning	hate cleaning other people's messes can't get kids to help wish Fred would support me more

Time	*Stress Level*	*Activities*	*Thoughts*
			Fred will probably insist on making love tonight
6:30 P.M.	8	supper	can't stand Fred's criticism kids won't do anything I'm tired all the time
9:30 P.M.	10	fought with Fred sewing/ mending	Fred doesn't understand kids take advantage of me Fred insists that I make love even when I don't feel like it Fred is unfair

Ann kept a similar stress log each day for two weeks. At the end of that time she reviewed her notes, looking for stress points in her life and for patterns in how she was feeling. Ann found, in general, that she was experiencing a great amount of stress. On the day excerpted above, thoughts about her Relief Society lesson (she is Spiritual Living leader), her children, Fred, and her general life situation were stressful. These same kinds of worries appeared consistently during the two weeks of recordings. A pattern also appeared showing that stress was highest in the morning and evening hours and on Sundays.

Procedure B: List and categorize stress points

Using the information collected over the two-week period, plus a general armchair analysis, Ann identified a long list of stress points in her life. A few of the items she listed are shown below.

Fred

— too insistent about sex (I worry about what he wants when he is nice to me).
— too critical — lots of put-downs
— doesn't seem to support me in disciplining the kids
— not home enough

Kids
— won't clean up after themselves without my yelling
— seem to fight a lot
— have to fight with them on chores

General
— too little time for myself
— too many demands on my time

Procedure C: Make plans to eliminate or reduce stress at each point

The next step was to consider how each stress area might be eliminated or reduced. Options included: (1) removing the stress, (2) removing self from the stress, (3) thinking about stress in a different way, and (4) grinning and bearing it. Ann made a plan of how she would handle every stress point listed. Obviously this was a large undertaking, and it took Ann several months to complete it. (One of the best ways to create stress is to try too hard to reduce it.)

Keep in mind that there are no universal "best" ways to reduce stress. What Ann decided to do worked for her, but for another person, Ann's solution might cause more stress than it eliminates. I should also point out that Ann used the trial-and-error approach. If her initial plan was not effective, she simply tried another.

The first problem Ann tackled was her sexual relationship with Fred. After considerable discussion with Fred, they decided to schedule lovemaking for particular nights. Exceptions were to be made for illness, vacations, and other occasions if they were agreed to in advance. Fred and Ann found that, for them, the advantages to this system outweighed the disadvantages. Fred was able to demonstrate his caring at other times without Ann misperceiving his intentions, which resulted in more trust and acceptance on both sides of the relationship. Both Fred and Ann found the situation to be more comfortable when they knew exactly what to expect sexually from one another.

Ann could not do much directly about Fred's frequent criticizing; but she did find that as the sexual issue was resolved and as she became less negative with Fred, the level of critical attack from him diminished. Ann, therefore, made it a goal not to be critical of Fred. She also decided that when he was being critical she would not try to defend herself (when she did it always resulted in an argument and more stress). Rather, she would repeat *to herself* several times: *I will not become a double victim by defending myself. I am a good person, and Fred knows it. His criticizing says more about his problems than about mine. I'm not perfect, but who says that I must be at this point?* If Fred's attacks got out of hand, as they sometimes had, she simply resolved to remove herself from the situation temporarily (visit a friend, go shopping, go for a walk).

Ann addressed each point on her stress list in a similar manner. She determined what could be done about the problem, tried the new solution, and then evaluated the results. Ann found that she was able to reduce much of the stress in her life. She also found that with a significant overall reduction in stress, she had plenty of reserve strength left to cope with troublesome problems which could not be changed and which simply had to be borne with a smile.

Little Stress Points Add Up to Big Ones

While large sources of stress often create great problems, small sources of stress have a cumulative effect and can be just as bothersome. Consider these relatively minor stress points in your stress analysis:

Lawn needs mowing.
Clothes need mending.
Sewing machine, automobile, etc., doesn't work properly.
You need the proper tool to complete a job.
The neighbor's dog barks at night.
The kids are noisy in church.

Sacrament meeting speakers are boring.
You forget names too easily.
You have no convenient, quiet place to study.
John/Mary keeps asking for favors.
Your office at work is too small.
The cost of gas is too high.
You can't find paper or a pencil when needed.
There is a constant need to run up and down stairs.
The phone constantly rings.

In most cases simple changes, such as having a secret cache of paper, unplugging the phone at certain times, buying a special tool, and mowing the lawn rather than worrying about it, are all that are necessary to reduce stress. The next chapter, on assertiveness, suggests how to handle the more difficult social stress points.

Stress for No Reason

Given the fact that each person has a limited capacity to tolerate stress safely and that life involves inevitable stress, it makes no sense at all for us to create stress in our minds. Yet we often do this when we establish unrealistic goals for ourselves, when we accept responsibility for that which we cannot control, and when we let guilt get out of hand. Another category of senseless stress involves worrying about the future. Planning for the future is wise, but spending energy dreading possible future outcomes is unproductive and can often cause additional stress.

Many people waste a lot of energy worrying about whether or not the plane will crash; a psychopath will break into the house at night; the stock market will crash; or an earthquake will devastate the city. All of these possible events basically are beyond our control and, therefore, beyond what we should concern ourselves with. You can do something about the kind of worker you are, the kind of person you are, the way you maintain your year's food supply, and the way you keep the commandments. If these things are in place or at least you are working on them, it really doesn't matter so much what happens in the world.

As Latter-day Saints we know more about the future of this world and, in one sense, have more basis for fear than do most other people. On the other hand, we also have a better understanding of God's dealings with men, which leads to more trust and faith in him. John A. Widtsoe, spoke in conference during World War II regarding fear and how it can be overcome.

> Fear, which "shall come upon every man," is the natural consequence of a sense of weakness, also of sin. Fear is a chief weapon of Satan in making mankind unhappy. He who fears loses strength for the combat of life, for the fight against evil. Therefore, the power of evil ever seeks to engender fear in human hearts. . . .
>
> He has expressly declared that man cannot stop his work on earth, therefore they who are engaged in the Lord's latter-day cause and who fear, really trust man more than God, and thereby are robbed of their power to serve.
>
> The key to the conquest of fear has been given through the Prophet Joseph Smith. "If ye are prepared ye shall not fear" (D&C 38:30). That divine message needs repeating today in every stake and ward. Are we prepared to surrender to God's commandments? In victory over our appetites? In obedience to righteous law? If we can honestly answer yes, we can bid fear depart. And the degree of fear in our hearts may well be measured by our preparation by righteous living, such as should characterize Latter-day Saints. (John A. Widtsoe, in Conference Report, April, 1942, pp. 33-34.)

Elder Widtsoe points out that those who have faith in God and who are prepared to keep his commandments (making a wholehearted effort, not necessarily being perfect at it) need not worry about events in the world. The worst thing that could be imagined, a nuclear holocaust, for example, is nothing to fear. Life would go on in spite of death. Those who have prepared themselves will be happy. Right will triumph, and all will be well with those who are on the Lord's side. So, then, what are we worried about?

The Worst-Possible-Outcome Ploy

If we can get comfortable with the worst possible outcome in any situation, then we have nothing to fear. If you are afraid of an intruder in the night, take reasonable precautions, such as installing deadbolts and window locks. Once done, forget it. Turning up the radio, leaving lights on in the house, or doing other abnormal things to try to feel more comfortable usually serve as cues that there is something to worry about, and increases rather than decreases fear.

But assume that you are not afraid to die or even to suffer physically. Certainly you don't want to die, and you don't want to get hurt; but at the same time you know that, no matter what happens to the body, all will be well with you in the long run. You are also convinced that you will be given strength to handle whatever happens in your life. Then, obviously, there is nothing to fear. In fact, becoming comfortable with the worst alternative is usually more effective in relieving fear than trying to convince yourself that the probability of the worst outcome is extremely remote. No matter how low the odds, some people keep reminding themselves, "But what if it *did* happen?"

Actually, the best strategy probably is to do both — to look at the odds and to become comfortable with the worst alternative. An appropriate self-talk in the situation described above would be similar to the following: *It will not happen. The odds of someone breaking in here and hurting me are much lower than the odds of my being hurt in a car accident, and I don't worry about that. And so what if it happens anyway? I have nothing to fear. I believe in God and in an eternal future. And I believe that all will be well with me in the long run. I also know that with God's help I can handle anything in the short run.* That type of thinking repeated over and over in the feared situation, while keeping other aspects of the environment normal, usually will reduce fear significantly.

This same strategy can be followed with other fears, such as fear of losing a job, fear of a major illness, or fear of flying. It is also useful in coping with small, mundane worries which have a cumulative effect and can lead to a significant stress problem. Some women, for example, worry that their homes are not clean enough for company. The worst thing that could happen in such cases is that guests will say to themselves, *What an untidy, lazy person she is*. But so what? Actually the guests probably will not even notice that the house is not as clean as it could be. If they do notice, they probably will feel glad that Sister Jones is so human after all, and they will feel much more comfortable about inviting her to their homes.

If the remote possibility does occur and the guests do leave saying what an untidy, lazy person their hostess is, it is hard to imagine why that would have to hurt (smart a little, yes — but hurt, no). Such comments are better indicators of the neurotic thinking of the guests than of the worth and value of the lady of the house. And, after all, what normally matters to guests is the way they are treated, not how clean the house is. If a person is so concerned about the way the house looks that he or she becomes apologetic, stiff, distant, or anxious, guests may well leave with negative feelings, but not because the house is untidy.

Pleasant Thoughts to Relax

Once we have identified the worst thing that could happen and have decided that it would not be so bad after all, then it is important to visualize the positive and to eliminate (or at least to minimize) the negative. If we are afraid of an intruder in the night, we need to imagine having a safe night's sleep which, of course, is infinitely more probable. If we fear that the plane we are flying in will crash, we need to visualize a safe arrival. In general, we need to imagine in some detail ourselves being successful in the situation that elicits fear. Points regarding how this can be done most effectively are given in chapter 9.

Chapter 9 also provides a description of simple relaxation exercises which are useful in reducing stress — which is, after all, inevitably a part of life.

Attention to Detail

Detail in our thinking is critical if we are to successfully follow the suggestion given above. If we are picturing our safe arrival on an airplane, for example, we need to imagine the scene in detail, as if we were watching it in a movie or on television; or, better yet, as if it were actually happening. We need to imagine facial expressions, comments, emotions, smells, sounds, decor, and clothing. Zoom in for imaginary close-ups of the action and then back off for a total look. Imagining the successful outcome in detail is much more helpful than simply letting the thought pass through your mind.

If your purpose is simply to rest your mind by picturing a pleasant scene, detail again is important. You need to try to hear the sound of the seagulls and the roar of the surf, to smell the sea air, and to feel the heat of the sun. Tuning in to detail is essential in turning the mind away from troublesome negative thoughts.

Whether your intent is to be more relaxed in general or at a specific time such as during a daily commute, attending to detail is useful. How do things work? What new thing can be seen in a common, often-viewed environment? What do the clouds look like? Which shrubs are in bloom? What does the air smell like today? I am amazed at the number of people who visit my office who do not know if there are clouds in the sky that day or not. These people are so turned inward to their own worries and concerns that they are missing much in life that could help them relieve some of their tension and stress.

Schedule Worry

Worry is almost never a productive use of energy, and several suggestions have been given here regarding how to reduce the number of things we worry about. Another way to reduce worry is to limit the time you invest in dealing with worrisome problems. It may sound ridiculous, but I counsel some people to schedule their worry time.

They set aside certain times during the day in which to concentrate on problems. When they are tempted to worry about a difficulty at other times, they deliberately postpone those thoughts to their "worry period." Often by the time the appointed hour has arrived, their "worry" has disappeared. When it has not, they ask themselves such questions as, *What can I do about it?* If they can think of some constructive solutions, they then begin to think of ways to implement them. If, on the other hand, they decide that there is nothing they can do about the problem, they give no further serious thought to it.

Stress and Productivity

The ideas and techniques presented above are useful in limiting and controlling stress. And given today's fast-moving world and its high-tension activities, such skills are necessary for comfortable living. You may be *worried*, however, about becoming so relaxed that motivation for achievement is reduced. Actually, the increased physical and emotional health possible with controlled stress adds to motivation and energy for productive living. If you are not convinced, by trying it out you will find, as have many others, that you can be free of excessive stress and also be maximally productive.

I Really Should Do That, But . . . 6

Some people create considerable stress for themselves by their seeming inability to get things done — in a word, procrastination. Procrastination means putting off things that really should be completed. Past chapters have warned against taking on too much responsibility; but there is also the danger in not taking on enough responsibility or of being irresponsible. When we leave some tasks undone we create inconvenience for ourselves or others, and often we prevent ourselves from accomplishing our desired goals.

Who among us has not at one time or another (perhaps consistently) put off developing an exercise program, or completing a year's supply of food (or writing this book?). Some of us procrastinate paying bills, answering letters, or keeping up the yard. We also may put off contacting that nonmember family down the street regarding their interest in the Church, or contacting a friend who may need a helping hand. When we procrastinate and fail to complete important tasks, we pay a high price. Friends, loved ones, and associates often are alienated by our irresponsible behavior; and we usually end up condemning ourselves severely, even brutally in many cases.

Paradoxically, a procrastinator generally condemns himself because he is *not* a lazy person, even though he may be so labeled by himself and others. Typically a procrastinator is converted to the work ethic and, therefore, is upset at his failure to complete certain tasks. He wants to do things; he is often an active, fast-moving person. Procrastination usually is limited to specific tasks or specific areas of a person's life. A lazy individual, on the other hand, is someone who is indisposed to exertion; he is indolent, sluggish, and slothful in general. Inactivity for the lazy person is a way of life in a broad sense, and that life-style creates little or no guilt for him.

The distinction between laziness and procrastination is important because of its implications for solving the problem. A lazy person needs to use strong language on himself in order to get moving; a procrastinator needs to avoid self-blame. Self-blame and thought, such as, *I'm a lazy, slothful person,* are chief contributors to procrastination. Those who condemn and criticize themselves increase the size of the task they are putting off because they now must also work through the negative emotion and loss of faith created by their self-condemnation. They also increase the inherently disagreeable nature of the task by associating with it negative feelings about themselves. In general, lazy people usually will respond best to pressure — a carrot-and-stick approach. On the other hand, procrastinators usually respond best to pressure removal — identifying the cause of the problem and removing the cause, rather than putting on more pressure to perform.

Causes of Procrastination

Four common causes of procrastination, with examples of each, are suggested below. Common rationalizations which prevent us from solving the problem are given next, followed by suggestions as to how procrastination can be overcome.

Cause 1: I must achieve more than others

Much procrastination is related to a high need for achievement. Someone who has a need to be best or first will often procrastinate or avoid assignments altogether if the probability is high that his effort will not be the best.

Tom kept putting off submitting his ideas at work. Although he was not aware of it, Tom was unconsciously afraid that the ideas submitted by his associates would be more creative than his. Tom's need to be best interfered with his own creative process. He prematurely dismissed many ideas because on the surface they did not appear exciting or grand enough. Tom also made the task into something so large that he had a difficult time in getting himself to work on it. And, finally, Tom held back from submitting the work he had completed because of his compulsive need to make it better.

Ellen, a senior in high school, kept procrastinating her homework. She had no problem with intellectual ability, as evidenced by the ingenious ways she invented to avoid submitting assignments. Her grades suffered, however, because she did little work, and what she did consisted of last-minute efforts. Her parents had a difficult time in believing that her need for achievement was too high, but so it was. Ellen had to be the best. When she was in elementary school she did very well. As she got older, competition increased and the probability of her doing better than others decreased. At that point Ellen began to back away from completing assignments.

When she turned work in late or gave it only a halfhearted effort, she had a built-in excuse for failing. *I could be great if I tried, but I don't want to try,* she rationalized. Her conclusion was safe, since it was never put to the test. If she studied hard and failed, she would be forced to admit that she wasn't the best. By not trying, she found it easier to believe that she could do it if she really wanted to.

Of course, the thing that both Tom and Ellen feared most — failing — was guaranteed by the way they went about trying to avoid and excuse failure.

Cause 2: It must be done perfectly

We put off doing some jobs because they involve a great deal of effort. Debbie has a sink full of dishes at all hours of the day and night. The problem, in part, is that when Debbie washes the dishes, she almost always ends up feeling compelled to clean the refrigerator, mop the floor, and take out the garbage. Since she is only vaguely aware of this tendency, Debbie cannot understand why she lets dishes pile up, and why she takes such a long time to do the job when she finally does get to it. Even though the task itself is a simple one, her perfectionistic orientation results in a complicated and energy-expensive proposition whenever she attempts to do the dishes or a similar job.

The same problem can occur when individuals refuse or procrastinate Church assignments. Most callings in the Church, like many other tasks in life, are open-ended. The sky is the limit in terms of how much time and energy one can put into these assignments. Those who feel compelled to devote themselves 100 percent to anything they attempt must, therefore, severely limit what they undertake. When pressed to serve, they may say yes but then procrastinate doing the assignment because of an overload of commitments to which they are already giving 100 percent.

A related problem exists for individuals who feel compelled to finish projects they have started before going on to others. Some people delay tasks indefinitely because there seems to be so little time to see the tasks through from start to finish.

Cause 3: I don't like it, them, or you

Hostility, often unrecognized, is another major cause of procrastination. Herb knows that he needs to lose weight, but he doesn't do so — primarily because he resents his wife's frequent complaints about how fat he is. Jerry should apply for his business license, but he has not done so — largely because he thinks the license requirement is a government scheme to take his money. Janet knows that she would like herself better and that her home environment would improve if she were more loving and less critical with her husband, but she keeps putting off improvements in this area — primarily because she assumes it would not be fair to be nice to him when he is being so rotten to her.

Hostility even goes so far, in some cases, that individuals put off self-improvement because they are angry with God. Some hold him accountable for what they feel is an unfair distribution of blessings. Feeling abused, rejected, and full of hate, they put off constructive problem-solving and then blame God for their unhappiness.

Cause 4: It hurts too much

In a useful book on procrastination, Albert Ellis and William Knaus point out that some people seem to have a low frustration tolerance (LFT, as they call it).[1] When we procrastinate tasks, we avoid present pain — but only in exchange for long-term pain. Fear of embarrassment in an awkward social situation often makes doing missionary work uncomfortable in the short run; but the effort can pay large dividends to the missionary in the long run. Going to school, taking tests, applying for a job, making new friends, exercising, dieting, investing, going to sacrament meeting, paying tithing — you name it — most things that are worthwhile in the long run can be uncomfortable at times in the short run. *Uncomfortable* may be too strong a word in some cases, but normally there are more pleasant immediate alternatives than the task procrastinated.

A person having LFT convinces himself that he cannot stand the pain or effort involved in bringing about desired goals. *I can't stand to do the dishes. I feel too uncomfortable to go to Church. I can't bear to sit here and read a book.* A procrastinator usually condemns himself to the point that the pain felt from procrastination probably hurts worse than the discomfort involved in completing the task. But the pain of procrastination

[1] Albert Ellis and William J. Knaus, *Overcoming Procrastination* (New York: Institute for Rational Living, 1977).

is experienced primarily in the longer term. At any given point it is probably more comfortable temporarily to delay the task.

Common Rationalizations

Ellis and Knaus also point to some common rationalizations that support procrastination. Read the following list and see if you have used similar reasoning in putting off important tasks.

1. I work best under pressure, so I will put off this task until the pressure is on.
2. I don't know how to get started or how to do the job properly.
3. I don't really want to do it.
4. It really doesn't matter if I get it done or not.
5. It will be easier if I am in the mood, so I'll wait until I feel more ready for it.
6. I can complete things successfully at the last minute — I've done it before, so why push?
7. Waiting until the last minute saves a lot of time and energy.
8. I could have done it sooner, but circumstances beyond my control prevented it.
9. If I do it now, I will never again have the chance to do what I would rather do at this time.
10. I have worked on this so long that I don't want to do it anymore.
11. No one cares about this, so I might as well put if off.

In order for rationalizations to be effective, they must be close to the truth or applicable in at least some situations. Many of the above statements are justifications for deciding not to do something at all (e.g., "No one cares about this"), and it is true that it really doesn't matter if some things are not done (4 above). But these statements are sometimes misapplied to tasks that really are important (such as spending time with one's spouse or children). And they can be overused or misapplied to too many tasks in general.

Rebutting the Rationalizations

Rationalizations lose their effectiveness when they are recognized for what they are and when counterlogic is used against them. Go back to the list above and see if you can identify the faulty thinking involved in each rationalization. Some suggestions, patterned after those from Ellis and Knaus, are given below. (Note: Assume that we are talking about completing what you feel is an important task.)

1. I work best under pressure, so I will put off this task until the pressure is on. Tasks may seem easier when done under pressure, but probably they are not. Effort may not last as long if put forth at the last minute because typically a late effort involves late hours, disruption in life-style, frustration in not being able to gather materials or information effectively, intense concentration, and, in general, a large expenditure of energy. It is hard to imagine how that kind of effort could be easier than completing the task ahead of schedule in a more relaxed manner. Certainly last-minute jobs will suffer in quality.

2. I don't know how to get started or how to do the job properly. Not knowing how to do the job is a good reason to find out how, but not a good reason to delay starting. Most tasks cannot be learned without practice. This means that we will not learn how to do the job until we start. Normally, a person is at a loss even to know the right questions to ask about a task until after he has had some experience with it.

3. I don't really want to do it. Once a decision has been made that completing an assignment will pay long-term dividends and that it should be done, not wanting to do it is irrelevant. All this means is that you had better start the job and get it over with as soon as possible. At least then it will be out of the way.

4. *It really doesn't matter if I get it done or not.* It is true that we have free agency and that no task *must be* completed. At the same time, you *will not* reap the benefits from certain experiences if those things are not done. If you've made the decision that the task should be completed, then the long-term advantages make the short-term disadvantage worthwhile.

5. *It will be easier if I am in the mood, so I'll wait until I feel more ready for it.* The problem in waiting for the right mood is that it may never come. Motivation for completing assignments and interest in them generally depend on becoming involved. Many thousands of would-be genealogists are waiting to get interested before they start; whereas, of course, interest usually comes only *after* they have become involved.

6. *I can complete things successfully at the last minute – I've done it before, so why push?* What appears to be good work, even though it was rushed, may be an illusion; it may be a good effort *considering* that it was done at the last minute. Even if you did successfully complete it, it probably could have been done in a more relaxed fashion without the high stress involved in late efforts.

7. *Waiting until the last minute saves a lot of time and energy.* Time may be saved by doing the job poorly, but there is no reason that a good effort should take any more time at one point than at another. In fact, early effort often takes less time and energy because of factors such as easier access to information, avoiding long lines, and working in conjunction with other tasks.

8. *I could have done it sooner but circumstances beyond my control prevented it.* Circumstances do interfere with plans, but we need to be sure that this is not simply an excuse. One of the reasons to complete assignments early is to allow for circumstances which may come up unexpectedly.

9. *If I do it now I will never again have the chance to do what I would rather do right now.* We normally make our opportunities; seldom do they simply happen. The chronic procrastinator usually does not make too many opportunities.

With a reasonable schedule and ordinary planning ability, we would rarely have a situation come up that represented a genuine once-in-a-lifetime opportunity.

10. I have worked on this so long that I don't want to do it anymore. This rationale, when used by a procrastinator, usually means that the job has been going on too long because he keeps putting it off. Without procrastination and under normal circumstances, the desire to complete a task increases the closer to its completion one gets. This is especially true if the task is an unpleasant one.

11. No one cares about this, so I might as well put it off. If the decision was made that the assignment is important, there is at least one person who cares — you! Others also are likely to benefit from its completion or be handicapped if it is not done.

Notice that the classic rationalization "there isn't enough time" is not included in the list. The reason for its exclusion is that it is usually a second-order thought, coming after one or more of the other rationalizations have been used.

Overcoming Procrastination — Changing Our Thinking

Two general approaches are useful in overcoming procrastination. The first is to change irrational conclusions about ourselves and the world which contribute to our putting off tasks. The second is to reinforce ourselves to be responsible. Each of these general approaches is described in more detail below.

In order to remove procrastination-inducing conclusions about ourselves and the world, we must first become aware of them. Which ones in the list of procrastinations and rationalizations have a familiar ring? What do you tell yourself before, during, and after putting off an important task? With a little awareness, you should be able to identify most of the problems in your thinking. The next step is to convert yourself to a different set of conclusions. A few suggestions regarding the thinking that you should convert to were given in the case of common rationalizations. More suggestions for changing thinking are given below with respect to the four major causes of procrastination outlined earlier.

Cause 1: I must achieve more than others

Why do we think that we must achieve more than others? Achievement is important but competition is not, at least not in connection with things that have eternal consequences. Apparently there are as many places in the celestial kingdom as will be needed for those who qualify. I am not in competition with others for a limited number of vacancies. Happiness, likewise, is available in unlimited quantities. If Jack is exceptionally happy, that in no way deprives me of an opportunity to be equally or more happy, nor does it in the least diminish my chances for happiness. Friendship, health, faith, hope, charity, knowledge, and wisdom are among other important goals that can be obtained without depriving others of their opportunity to have the same advantages in equal measure. In fact, I can't think of a genuinely important thing that can be had only at the expense of someone else.

Then why do some people try so hard to be better than others? Some people put so much energy into running farther, hitting harder, and racing faster than others that recreational pursuits become stress producing rather than relaxing. Insistence on winning arguments or "being understood" (which usually means being agreed with) is a common cause of marital strife. Having a fancier car, wearing better clothes, having a bigger house, or gaining other evidence of status become all-consuming goals for some people. Why?

Lack of real self-esteem is the most common answer. Those who lack faith in their own abilities and who lack understanding of their own intrinsic worth often seek outward evidence of acceptance. But it never works. There is always someone with a bigger house or more money. Each compliment received from others or each new possession acquired may create a momentary sense of security, but that sense vanishes quickly, leaving the individual hungry for another compliment or another purchase to prove his worth yet again.

Several aspects of our society contribute to the "need" people have to be better than others: (1) conditional acceptance from parents (you are okay only if you do great things); (2) a materialistic emphasis by advertising and other mass media; and (3) a competitive spirit nurtured in schools, sports, and the business world. But no matter why or where the idea originates, it is an irrational one.

Today is Monday. Bruce is the head of a large corporation and feels a sense of importance and worth. But on Tuesday, the following day, he loses his job; now he feels totally inadequate. Yet Bruce is the same person both days. Nothing intrinsical about him has changed, only his circumstances are different. The acquisition of material comforts does not determine self-worth. A person who drives a luxury car is no better on that account than a person who drives a subcompact. Having more of something materially attractive does not make one a better person than someone who has less.

I recommend to procrastinators (and to all of us) that we convince ourselves of the following: (1) nothing worth having can be had at the expense of someone else; (2) I am not in competition with anyone for happiness in this life or the next; (3) I am a person of worth and value, with or without material possessions and status; (4) doing my best, being myself, and enjoying myself (without breaking the commandments) are what really count. As Wayne Dyer has pointed out, "No, coach, winning isn't everything or the only thing; it is only *a* thing." (Wayne W. Dyer, *Pulling Your Own Strings* [New York: Thomas Crowell Co., 1978], p. 161.) Winning may be fun and exciting, but it does *not* make us better than the person who loses.

Cause 2: It must be done perfectly

Most of the tasks we perform on a daily basis need to be completed, but they don't have to be done perfectly. Take doing the dishes, for example. Generally, it isn't necessary to carefully scrub each item to a sparkling shine. Simply rinsing the food off and sterilizing the utensils will get the job done (and these days most dishwashers will do that for you). The dishes can be completed without mopping the floor, cleaning the toaster, and washing all the appliances. Doing the job well is important, but being overly thorough is unnecessary and often is the reason for procrastination.

Starting a project is also important, even if you have insufficient time to finish it without interruptions. A long-delayed two-day job should be started even if you have only an hour to work on it. If that means hauling out materials, fine. At least the supplies needed to complete the project will then be gathered in one place. And perhaps having the unfinished task in the garage or on the desk in plain sight will encourage continued effort to complete it.

We are less likely to procrastinate if we understand (1) that we can work on jobs a little bit at a time and (2) that jobs do not have to be done to the extreme.

Cause 3: I don't like it, them, or you

When we say, "I don't like it," we are allowing anger to be in control. We need to recognize the anger and admit responsibility for the inaction. When we delay out of spite, it is easy to blame the object of our anger for our delay. *If it were not for Laura's constant complaining about it, I could lose weight. If the government were not corrupt, I would be happy to pay taxes. I won't pay tithing as long as that man is bishop.* In each case, the object of one's anger is thought to be the real reason for procrastination when, in fact, it is not.

When you are tempted to fall into this trap, apply the "double-victim" notion described earlier. *Yes, it is unfair of Laura to keep nagging me about my excess weight. But why should I continue to suffer from overweight because of Laura's problem? I can't stop Laura from complaining, but I can stop letting her criticism affect* my *behavior as it has.* If we deprive ourselves of a desirable goal out of spite, we become double victims; and we have allowed someone else's behavior, over which we have no control, to determine our behavior.

It is important to admit that we don't like something that

has happened; but we also need to be sure that we don't let that unhappy event or situation control the decisions we make. *I will be the kind of spouse I can be proud of, even if my husband treats me rotten. If I am not, I simply make matters worse for myself than they need to be. I can't change him, but I can be comfortable within myself in spite of him. Even if it is unfair, why make it more unfair by overreacting?*

Cause 4: It hurts too much

Once we convince ourselves that we cannot bear the immediate discomfort necessary in reaching long-term goals, movement toward those goals stops. Obviously, then, in order to avoid procrastination we must convince ourselves that (1) in the long run the rewards are worth the temporary effort or inconvenience involved, and that (2) we can tolerate the short-term pain. Believing that the rewards justify the effort is usually the easy part. Deciding that the effort can be endured is more difficult. This is especially true in our culture where the have-it-now philosophy is advanced by everything from the credit industry to the pharmaceutical companies. (Take a pill and feel better *now*. Fly now and pay later.)

Those unable to wait for gratification (those with low frustration tolerance) can get by in the short run, but there is always the long run to consider. Someone once pointed out that the problem with the "eat, drink, and be merry, for tomorrow we die" philosophy is that we don't die tomorrow. We go on living and suffering the consequences of our shortsighted hedonism. This is, of course, even more true when we understand that life continues after death and that all inadequate living eventually leads to negative consequences.

The possibility of achieving long-term goals increases if we remember the following points: (1) I can tolerate almost anything. (Certainly I can put up with a boring book required in my school work; or certainly I won't die if I ask Julie out, and she says no.) (2) I must put aside short-term interests if I want something in the long term. (High school and college graduation depends on my reading "boring" books; or I must risk rejection if I want friends.) (3) With a little planning I can make my life interesting and comfortable while I work on long-term goals. (I must study tonight, but I can go out tomorrow.)

Reinforcing Responsible Behavior

We win a big part of the battle against procrastination when we identify and modify our thoughts that contribute to it. The victory can be complete if, at the same time, we reinforce more responsible behavior. Doing so makes the short-term discomfort more palatable and less likely to obstruct action. A few simple approaches to overcoming procrastination through reinforcement are suggested below.

Reinforce action. Identify special enjoyments, such as talking to a friend, listening to music, reading a magazine, or taking a nap. Now, identify a task that has been procrastinated and contract with yourself to work on the project on a given schedule. Immediately after working on the task, but only after working on it as planned, reward yourself with a special enjoyment.

Punish inaction. Try reinforcing yourself first; if that does not seem to work, punishing yourself for not working on a procrastinated task can be effective. When using punishment (or positive reinforcement, for that matter), it is often wise to have a second party responsible for applying the penalty (or reward) — it is too easy to renege on promises to oneself. For example, you might undertake that, if you have not completed a long-delayed project by a certain date, for a specified period you will do a certain household chore which normally is done by your spouse.

Work with friends and associates. Many people who have procrastinated exercise programs have found the motivation they need by working with a friend. Meeting another person every morning at a certain time will often provide the incentive needed to get one's back off the mattress rather than getting back on the mattress. Shared goals with deadlines and shared rewards or punishments can also be effective incentives. Working together is a chief factor in the success of weight control groups, Alcoholics Anonymous, and other self-help programs.

Schedule. Inertia is a genuine problem for procrastinators. Yet once they begin a project, they often find it relatively easy to keep working on it. Try beginning a project with the intent to spend five or ten minutes on the task. At the end of that time make a decision about whether to continue working for another five- or ten-minute segment. Use this scheduling until the project is finished or until some predetermined amount of time has elapsed. Scheduling specific times to work on tasks can also help break inertia. Decisions about what to work on and when to work on it can be a daylong, confusing problem if you lack an advance plan.

Remind yourself. Notes to oneself posted in places where procrastination is likely to take place can be helpful. A note on the refrigerator, telephone, television, or bed can help remind us of our intent to complete certain projects.

Avoiding Blame

Undoubtedly, self-blame is a chief contributor to procrastination. Calling oneself a lazy good-for-nothing only increases the probability of procrastinating. Success is more likely if the causes for delaying tasks are understood and removed. Remember also that improvement is not a simple one-step proposition. Self-improvement almost always involves going a few steps backward in the process of taking many paces forward. Unfortunately, many people panic when they fall back a step or two, and then they begin to chastize themselves more than ever. Don't! With patience and consistency we can succeed. Impressive, splashy, miraculous improvement is not necessary. In fact, such change often is more difficult to maintain than slower, measured progress.

Assertively Avoiding Problems Rather Than Creating Them

7

Many Latter-day Saints whom I see professionally are confused as they compare the emphasis on assertiveness (as shown in psychological literature) with gospel teachings. Some advocates of individual assertiveness almost seem to suggest a callous disregard for the feelings of others: "I'm going to do it my way, and if you don't like it — tough!" At least practicing these assertion principles may result in that approach. A certain rebelliousness against order and rule is also an underlying theme in some writing: "If you don't see a reason for it, don't do it." (Adam, on the other hand, was commended for obeying, even when he did not know how doing so would be in his best interest — see Moses 5). People note too that following suggestions by assertiveness trainers can often lead to putting would-be manipulators in their places by putting them down.

Contrast these assertive behaviors with the Savior's instructions: "And blessed are the meek, for they shall inherit the earth" (3 Nephi 12:5). "And blessed are all the peacemakers, for they shall be called the children of God" (3 Nephi 12:9). "But behold I say unto you, love your enemies, bless them that curse you, do good to them that hate you, and pray for them who despitefully use you and persecute you'' (3 Nephi 12:44).

Actually, most psychologists and counselors advocating personal assertiveness do not recommend a callous, insensitive approach when advancing one's own interests. Pushy, overly aggressive, critical, and stubborn behavior creates far more stress in life than it eliminates, which is, no doubt, one reason why the Lord has counseled against such behavior. But it is also true that one can assertively approach the world without offending gospel principles.

In fact, Jesus Christ clearly demonstrated that, in the best sense of the term, he was ''his own person.'' At times he ignored certain religious rules and customs that were merely contrivances of men; for example, certain restrictions regarding Sabbath activities or keeping company with publicans and sinners. The Savior told the truth, even if some were offended by it; and he refused to be manipulated into feeling guilty when he had not sinned. For example, his comment to his mother when she apparently scolded him for staying behind in the temple was not defensive, but was a gentle reminder: ''Wist ye not that I must be about my Father's business?'' (Luke 2:49). When religious leaders of the day accused him of blasphemy, he calmly and confidently told the truth about himself in spite of their railings and accusations.

Even as Jesus refused to be manipulated into sin or self-depreciation, and even as he told the truth with confidence, an overriding love and concern for his fellowmen was evident. It is interesting, for example, that he did not always say everything that might be said. His comment to the woman taken in adultery was simply ''Neither do I condemn thee: go, and sin no more'' (John 8:11). Whereas, he would have been correct, but perhaps at that moment insensitive, to comment on the evils of committing adultery and the danger of losing exaltation. In fact, nothing Jesus Christ did was insensitive or malicious. People, on occasion, hurt themselves by their reactions to the truths he spoke, but he did not hurt anyone himself. He was forthright, courageous, and independent, but always with the best interests in mind of those with whom he related. (Keep in mind that sometimes it is in a person's best *long-term* interest to be told a fact that they find uncomfortable in the short term.) In short, Christ was effectively assertive.

The following are examples of situations in which we often fail to act assertively. A rationale is provided in each case for why an assertive action is in the individual's best interest and how the recommended action is compatible with the Savior's teachings. Several of the points made in this section are modifications of ideas found in Wayne Dyer's best-seller *Pulling Your Own Strings* which is a good summary of many of the principles currently advanced in assertiveness training.

Situation 1: A relative or friend wants to talk to you when you are busy

Inadequate Response: Go ahead and talk with him, but then worry about what isn't getting done and become resentful of the other person for "taking" your time.

Better Response: Simply say that you are busy at the moment with something that can't be put off and that you will call or talk later.

Rationale: The gospel involves loving others, which is extremely difficult to do if they frequently are frustrating us. Confused nonverbal and verbal messages probably will be sent in such cases, and these could be misread by the other person as a rejection of the individual rather than as a rejection of the interruption. If we continually give in to frustration, the probability of our "blowing up" and saying unkind, hurtful things increases.

Situation 2: A relative demands compliments, attention, gifts, or he or she gets hurt feelings

Inadequate Response: Try to meet the demand for compliments, attention, or gifts; or avoid the relative altogether.

Better Response: Refuse to give compliments, attention, or gifts when demanded but, in general, interact with the relative in a kind, considerate manner.

Rationale: Attention or love addicts are never satisfied. A "fix" will result in a brief positive feeling, but the next compliment must be bigger or come earlier. Two sons I counseled were manipulated into buying a house for their mother, who then was dissatisfied — the paint was the wrong color, the yard was too small, etc. Trying to satisfy an attention seeker's need is virtually impossible because the need always grows.

The gospel involves our caring about our fellowman and trying to do what is in his best interest. We do the attention addict no good by feeding his habit. Compliments that are engineered usually are not meaningful to the recipient anyway. What is helpful is a natural, caring relationship in which compliments and attention are given naturally and freely. This is possible only if attention is given when it is not demanded. Of course, in a close relationship not giving attention and compliments altogether is as unnatural as trying too hard to give them.

Situation 3: Someone puts down your opinion or criticizes the way you do something

Inadequate Response: Blaming oneself, changing opinions or behavior simply to make someone else happy, becoming defensive, angry, or hostile.

Better Response: Consider the criticism — change your behavior if appropriate, or forget the negative comment if it appears to have little or no merit. An appropriate response in the latter case is, "You may be right, but personally I prefer to believe or do this."

Rationale: In 3 Nephi 12:25 we read, "Agree with thine adversary quickly while thou art in the way with him, lest at any time he shall get thee, and thou shalt be cast into prison." Since the Lord would not be instructing us to be dishonest (to agree even when we don't agree), the directive must be that we not make a big issue out of negatives from other people. Pass them off. Otherwise, if we become defensive, we soon become hostile, and what initially was a small issue becomes a very large problem.

Situation 4: You want to tell children, spouse, parents, siblings, or friends that you love them

Inadequate Response: Let embarrassment get in the way and avoid honestly expressing your feelings.

Better Response: Let the positive feelings out, however awkwardly you feel you are doing it.

Rationale: A rationale is probably not needed here. Few people would argue with the value of expressing positive feelings. The situation is included as a reminder that lack of assertiveness leads to more than simply suffering negative outcomes unnecessarily. Fear of asserting ourselves blocks natural, positive behaviors as well.

Situation 5: Your spouse unexpectedly changes plans, causing a conflict with your plans

Inadequate Response: Go along with your spouse's plans, but then make him or her pay for your inconvenience by being critical and angry.

Better Response: Go along with the spouse's plans if you can do so comfortably. Otherwise, stick with your original plans.

Rationale: The issue is not whether to be kind to your spouse, but rather to do what is kindest. It does not seem to be particularly virtuous to sacrifice your personal plans to accommodate someone else's and then to resent the other person for the disruption. Likewise, it would not be useful to make a big issue out of the situation: "You always do this to me. Why can't you be sensitive enough to plan things better!" Inconvenience is a part of life. Partners who are insensitive at times are a part of life. Simplicity is the key.

Situation 6: Your spouse demands sexual encounters

Inadequate Response: Always give in, but then resent your partner.

Better Response: Refuse to respond to the demand, but indicate an interest at other times.

Rationale: Self-mastery not self-indulgence is a major theme of the gospel. There is no scriptural imperative indicating that a spouse should always be available to his or her partner on demand. The apostle Paul, for one, however, suggested that the sexual relationship is an important feature in a healthy marriage (see 1 Corinthians 7:2-5).

Sometimes a problem in this area can be resolved if the less interested partner refuses when pressure is applied, but then expresses interest within a relatively short time afterward when feeling less pressured. Differences in sexual interest are so common that some sort of compromise is usually required. A relationship is out of balance if things are done primarily the way one spouse likes them. Out-of-balance relationships are like out-of-balance tires — they wear unevenly and many soon blow out.

Situation 7: You are called to a Church position, but feel overwhelmed by the assignment or are strongly negative toward it

Inadequate Response: Automatically reject the calling; or accept it and then do nothing but complain.

Better Response: Voice all of your concerns honestly and carefully and ask the calling authority to reconsider. If the call is extended in spite of your concerns, it is probably best to accept it, at least on a trial basis.

Rationale: There are cases in which a Church assignment will conflict with higher priorities to self or family of which the calling authority is not aware. But, under normal circumstances, if you explain the situation to the leader extending the call he will usually rescind it. If he doesn't, and you still feel very strongly about not taking the assignment, it may be better to decline the call. (This assumes of course that you have done your best to obtain the guidance of the Spirit in the matter.) Certainly it is preferable to say no rather than to take the assignment and then provide little or no service.

Remember, however, that in many cases resistance to Church callings is based on fear regarding one's ability to perform; or, conversely, on a feeling that the calling does not use one's abilities effectively. In other cases the resistance to serving is purely selfish. In such situations it is better to go ahead with the calling, seeking the Lord's guidance in the spirit of Nephi's counsel (see 2 Nephi 32:9). The long-term advantage of service is worth what initially may seem to be the short-term discomfort of the call.

Situation 8: Someone in the Church asks you to do a favor or to take part in a project, but doing so would cause a serious inconvenience

Inadequate Response: Say yes, but then resent the person for asking.

Better Response: Indicate that prior commitments will not allow you to help.

Rationale: Service and consecration are important concepts of the gospel. They also can be useful contributors to good mental health. Service can help people forget their own problems while it nourishes self-esteem and self-confidence.

Sometimes the problem is that we forget to put ourselves on the list of service recipients. We can go further faster if we pace ourselves and if we are reasonable about our commitments. It is unreasonable under normal circumstances to always or usually say no to unofficial service requests; but one cannot always say yes either. Actually, your not being available on occasion may force those looking for help to contact someone new who genuinely needs the opportunity to serve.

Situation 9: Others try to put their responsibilities onto you

Inadequate Response: Accept the responsibility, and then worry about it and/or resent the person passing the responsibility.

Better Response: Indicate that you will do what you can to help, but that you will not accept the other person's responsibility.

Rationale: Individual accountability is a major theme of the gospel. ''We believe that men will be punished for their own sins, and not for Adam's transgression (second Article of Faith). A logical extension of this statement is to assume that you will also be free of the transgressions of John, James,

Mary, and Joan, and of everyone else except yourself. We each will be held accountable only for that over which we have been given control — ourselves, our talents, our abilities, our callings, and so on. We will be held accountable for our families and those who come under the influence of our stewardships, but only in terms of how *we* live our lives and what kind of examples we set.

In spite of this fact, others often try to get us to accept responsibility for their problems. And the more responsiblity we accept, the more is dumped our way. Your spouse or friend may try to make you responsible for his or her happiness. Teachers try to make parents responsible for the behavior of children in the classrooms. Children try to get parents to solve sibling conflicts by intervening in their behalf. A supervisor may try to blame you for a problem actually generated by his own poor planning. And so it goes. Violent opposition to these unreasonable attempts to transfer responsiblity is unnecessary. The simple response, "I will do what I can to help, but I see this as basically your responsibility," usually makes the point.

Situation 10: Smoke from a cigarette is making you uncomfortable

Inadequate Response: Suffer angrily in silence.

Better Response: Point out the problem and ask for the smoker's cooperation.

Rationale: The scriptures advocate meekness, which some define as being overly submissive, easily imposed upon, spineless, and spiritless. But in the scriptural context the term refers to patience, mildness, gentleness, and kindness. Pointing out the problem and asking for a smoker's cooperation can be done with kindness, mildness, and gentleness. In fact, kindly requesting cooperation seems considerably more Christlike than saying nothing but fuming internally about how you would like to shove that blankety-blank cigarette down the idiot's throat! Patience becomes important if the request for cooperation is not well received. If, for example, you are told, "If you don't like the smoke, move!" then pushing the issue would do no one any good.

Of course, it is also possible to become angry and to insist on cooperation in an unkind, insensitive manner. For instance: "Can't you read the sign, stupid?" or "Thanks for helping me get cancer." Such comments generally are too sarcastic to elicit cooperation from the smoker. The main goal of assertive living is to reduce stress, not to create it.

The situation described above is one of many situations in which others are unaware of or insensitive to our discomfort. A neighbor's dog barking, frequent impositions by friends, and shoes left in the hallway are examples of such irritations in daily living. If we do not express our discomfort, responsibility for the continuation of the situation is partly with us. Once we have made our discomfort known, responsibility shifts totally to the other person. If, after being told of our feelings, the other person still will not correct the situation, we must be patient. We have the option of changing it ourselves (wherein this is possible) or deciding that it is not important. As suggested earlier, making a scene, manipulating, or trying to force someone else to feel responsible or bad is always counterproductive and stress-producing.

Situation 11: An authority figure (supervisor, bureaucrat) demands that you do something that you consider unreasonable

Inadequate Response: Conform to the demand without questioning the authority figure.

Better Response: State your feelings in a kind but direct manner. If the demand is not changed to your satisfaction and the issue is important, take it to the next level of authority for resolution.

Rationale: The Prophet Joseph Smith recorded, "We have learned by sad experience that it is the nature and disposition of almost all men, as soon as they get a little authority, as they suppose, they will immediately begin to exercise unrighteous dominion" (D&C 121:39). The Lord's instruction to the

Saints who were subjected to such unrighteous dominion was to "importune for redress, and redemption, by the hands of those who [were] placed as rulers and [were] in authority over [them]" (D&C 101:76). I don't think it stretches the principle too far to apply it to situations in which our everyday rights and common sense are being trammeled by bureaucrats or other authority figures.

My wife and I once took a coupon to a motel, expecting to receive half price on accommodations as advertised on the coupon offer. The clerk indicated that management had changed hands and that the coupon was no longer being honored. "Under no circumstances can I accept this coupon," he replied. Trying hard to be civil and not argumentative, we pointed out that not honoring the coupon was, in our opinion, unreasonable (not to mention bad business). It was obviously a violation of advertised conditions. When the clerk remained adamant, we asked to see the manager. He arrived shortly, and after a brief discussion with us he decided to honor the coupon (although quite grudgingly).

The concept, again, is to state the complaint or request in a reasonable, nonthreatening manner; and if that fails, to take the matter over the head of the authority figure in charge if the issue seems to warrant doing so. If this fails, rely on patience, steadiness, endurance, and perserverance — it is no use becoming a double victim by over-reacting. (If we had been unable to secure the accommodations as per the coupon, my wife and I would have found another place to stay, but we would not have let the incident ruin our trip.)

The Principle of Kindness

One theme running through the examples given above is kindness and civility. Condemning or criticizing another individual is not necessary (even if you feel you have a right to be angry). Quiet resolve, respectful disagreement, and the absence of hostility, defensiveness, and argumentativeness are all characteristics of effective assertiveness.

Purposely overlooking problems is often not in the best interest of all concerned. Frequently the kindest thing to do in the long run is to point out error and to insist, within the limits of ethical and legal considerations, that the error be rectified. Many of those who have been subject to the Church court system, for example, will testify that firm action on the Church's part was painful to endure at the time but very much in the individual's long-term best interest.

The Principle of Forthrightness

A second major factor in effective assertiveness is forthrightness — clarity in communication. The "better response" examples suggested in the previous situations make the position of the victim clear. People who have a problem in asserting themselves often resort to innuendo and nonverbal communication to make their point. Unfortunately, indirect communication frequently is not received at all, or it is misperceived. Rather than making furtive glances at a smoker and then at the no smoking sign, hoping that the smoker will get the message, we should be forthright, which generally is more effective. Tell him directly that the smoke is causing a problem for you and that you would appreciate his consideration.

Lack of clear communication is most common in intimate relationships. Husbands and wives do get adept at "reading" one another's nonverbal cues, but it is easy to get overconfident. Many messages supposedly sent by nonverbal cues never get there. Even worse, many spouses assume that they need not communicate their wishes or needs at all. *If he loved me, he would understand* is a common but thoroughly wishful conclusion. What we would like or what we don't like needs to be communicated in clear, nonthreatening terms. When we convey our needs with kindness, the receiver rarely feels threatened. It is only when we start demanding and accusing that the receiver becomes defensive.

The Principle of Courage

Presenting oneself assertively in the world takes courage and self-confidence. It is difficult to always follow the "better response" option in the situations described in this chapter. Most of us are afraid to assert ourselves in at least some situations; for many people, passivity and noninvolvement are a way of life. Three basic fears that get in the way of assertiveness are fear of being rejected, fear of meeting a confrontation, and fear of making a mistake.

Fear of being rejected is often the main culprit in lack of assertiveness in interpersonal relationships. Faye is an attractive, personable lady, but she has a long history of short-term, disturbed relationships with men. She is so afraid that she will be rejected by a boyfriend that she seldom commits herself to a relationship; and the few times that she did commit herself, she became exceptionally jealous. She compared herself with other women, lost the competition (in her view), and became convinced that her boyfriend would soon reject her for someone else. At the slightest hint of the boyfriend losing interest, she rejected him — thus beating him to the punch and avoiding the "inevitable." The results of this action are twofold: a relatively unhappy life for Faye, and the absence of a long-term relationship with a man.

What is Faye afraid of? Being alone and feeling rejected. What happens to Faye as a result of her fears? She is alone and feels rejected. Ironically, what she fears most she creates herself as a result of being afraid. She feels more emotion in anticipation of a dreaded event than she feels when it actually arrives — if it ever does. Faye tells herself that she can't cope with rejection and must, therefore, avoid it at all costs. But, in fact, she experiences rejection (in her mind) in every relationship, and she is actually well practiced at coping with it. If she understood this, and if she trusted herself to be able to handle whatever happened in a relationship, she would have nothing to fear. She could assertively seek out, commit herself to, and maintain a stable relationship.

In general, if we feel confident in ourselves and in our ability to handle whatever response we receive from another, we can be effectively assertive in making our wants and wishes known. As we do so, we actually increase the probability of being accepted and of being treated with respect by others. Confidence breeds acceptance. Except for those people who wish to capitalize on our lack of confidence by manipulating us, or those who also feel inferior and unsure of themselves, our lack of confidence usually leads people to respond cautiously and to move away from us.

Fear of confrontation also contributes to a lack of effective assertiveness. If the smoker rudely refuses to cooperate with your request, it is not necessary to make an issue out of it and to extend the confrontation. "Thank you, anyway" or some similar comment normally will serve to pass it off. If a spouse angrily responds to your suggestion, you need not become defensive or hostile and argue about it. You might respond with: "I'm not demanding or condemning, I'm just asking. You don't have to agree, I'm just giving my opinion." These or similar neutral comments may defuse the situation. Certainly, if a negative, hostile confrontation does ensue, it would take both your cooperation and your involvement. If you can control your responses, why fear confrontation?

The keys to being assertive without having negative confrontations lie in (1) the principle of kindness — that is, making your point in a sensitive and caring manner; and (2) in the principal of patience — not pushing or insisting once it is obvious that cooperation will not be forthcoming.

With respect to the fear of making mistakes — life is a risk, and learning requires risk. We cannot live life comfortably and assertively until we become convinced that mistakes are something to be learned from and that, so long as they are not sins, they are not something to be feared. Certainly, chronic fear of failure guarantees failure, which makes the consequence of fearing mistakes greater than the consequence of the error itself.

Line Upon Line

As with so much in life, applying these ideas is easier talked about than done. Do not expect to become effectively assertive overnight. Plan on assessing where you are at the moment and making consistent, measured progress in this area. For some the goal should be to add kindness and patience to an already assertive life-style. For others, risking open communication and standing up for one's rights need to be added to the kindness and patience already possessed. For most of us the goal will be to improve in both respects.

It Works Only if You Work

8

Ideas presented in previous chapters can be powerful aids in coping with life. But, as suggested at the outset, this book will help you reduce problems in your life only if the principles discussed are applied. Many people I deal with are looking for a magic pill that solves all of life's problems. Alas, no magic elixir exists, nor will one ever be discovered. Even the gospel is not a magic pill, although sometimes it is viewed as such. Several people I know joined the Church thinking that it would solve all of their problems, but they became discouraged and fell away when it became obvious that the magic lay in application of gospel principles, not in mere Church membership.

The exercises and suggestions in this book are designed to make theory practical. By completing the assignments recommended, you can internalize the concepts involved; and once internalized, the new concepts will control your feelings and behavior as certainly as did the old. This chapter discusses some apparent contradictions in previous chapters, and gives a description of the "personal scientist" approach. The final chapter gives techniques for developing more effective coping skills.

Moderation in All Things

Excess in any direction often creates problems. Too much concern or misdirected concern about perfection is counterproductive (chapter 1); at the same time, too little concern is equally debilitating (chapter 6). We often assume responsibility for things we should not (chapter 2), but may fail to assume responsibility for those we should (chapter 3). Guilt is useful up to a point, but when taken to extremes it can cause more problems than it solves (chapter 4). Reducing stress is important for us all (chapter 5), although we must be willing to tolerate short-term stress in return for long-term rewards (chapter 6). A certain amount of assertiveness is essential to productive living, but one can be too assertive (chapter 7).

Any apparent contradictions in previous chapters can be reconciled by understanding that extremes typically are counterproductive at either end of the continuum; it is the extreme that I am warning against. Not being much concerned about achievement leads to problems, but then so does being overconcerned. Being unassertive is against one's best interest, but so is always insisting on getting one's way. Similarly, other good things (such as guilt) become bad when pushed too far.

How does one find that elusive middle ground? Many people refuse self-improvement goals out of fear that they will then become too extreme. For example, "If I become more assertive, maybe I will become callous, insensitive, and unchristian." Actually, it doesn't happen that way, at least not beyond an initial adjusting period. (Spouses and others will often complain as you initiate self-improvement goals; but usually a spouse complains in order to protect the status quo, and the complaint has no merit.) People whose behavior is at one end of a continuum have so much natural resistance to the other end that they will almost always adjust their behavior to a point considerably this side of the behavior they reject. Certainly if their behavior adjustments do not work, they can always make other changes.

In determining whether we have found the proper point between the extremes, we can always use the test question: What effect does our attitude and/or behavior have on us? And we can profitably link this with Mormon's counsel:

> Wherefore, take heed, my beloved brethren, that ye do not judge that which is evil to be of God, or that which is good and of God to be of the devil.
>
> For behold, my brethren, it is given unto you to judge, that ye may know good from evil; and the way to judge is as plain, that ye may know with a perfect knowledge, as the daylight is from the dark night.
>
> For behold, the Spirit of Christ is given to every man, that he may know good from evil; wherefore, I show unto you the way to judge; for everything which inviteth to do good, and to persuade to believe in Christ, is sent forth by the power and gift of Christ; wherefore ye may know with a perfect knowledge it is of God. (Moroni 7:14-16.)

In my opinion, some of us get the signals confused. For example, some people feel that they are motivated by the Spirit to push themselves harder, further, and faster. But the consequences of their doing so frequently include a more negative outlook; perhaps less interest in the Church, and more bickering and critical behavior within the family. In some cases the changed life-style leads to immorality, immobilization, or illness. Seeing these consequences, I think Mormon would suggest that the motivation is probably coming from the devil and not from God.

You should keep three important conclusions in mind, then, as you undertake self-improvement goals designed to bring you proper control of your life and the correct approach to responsibility and assertiveness: (1) the ideal probably is closer to the middle, than to either extreme; (2) don't allow fear of becoming too extreme prevent you from moving toward your goal; and (3) evaluate the appropriateness of what you are doing on the basis of its consequences. Are you happy? Does the change move you toward Christlike attitudes and behavior? Is the outcome for you positive and forward-looking?

As a final caution on this subject, we should remember that even inherently good things, such as home evenings and sacrament meetings, can have negative consequences if approached from the wrong perspective. A dry, lecture-type home evening forced on children can do more damage than good. A divorced man may feel worse after attending sacrament meeting because he assumes that ward members are rejecting him or that he doesn't belong at church without a family. In these cases, the problem is not in the home evenings or sacrament meetings *per se,* but in how each is approached. Eliminating the problem in such instances means modifying the approach, not avoiding the potentially good thing altogether.

The Personal Scientist Approach

Since finding and keeping the right spot between extremes is so difficult, living life comfortably requires continual awareness of what we are doing and what are the consequences of our behavior. One method for gaining this awareness is the personal scientist approach explained in a useful book on weight control by Michael J. and Kathryn Mahoney.[1] These authors draw a parallel between the problem-solving approach of a research scientist and that of someone interested in developing self-control. The problem-solving approach involves defining the problem, collecting data, identifying patterns, narrowing options, comparing data, and revising or replacing hypotheses. Each of these steps to problem solving is described below.

But first, let's decide what self-control is and what it is not. Self-control is *not* an individual trait that is genetically determined. It is not a part of a person's makeup. Those who say that they lack self-control are usually mistaken. They may

---

[1]Michael J. Mahoney and Kathryn Mahoney, *Permanent Weight Control: A Total Solution to the Dieter's Dilemma* (New York: W. W. Norton & Co., 1976).

have trouble in controlling specific behaviors, but they normally do exhibit control in many, if not most, areas of their life. Self-control is a skill. It exists to a lesser or greater degree at any point in time and with respect to various issues; but it can be improved, just as can one's ability to shoot baskets or hammer nails.

Those who define self-control as a genetically determined component of oneself lose motivation and confidence to improve. *What's the use? I can't do it because I have no self-control.* Those who see self-control as a skill that can be developed find motivation to push forward. *I haven't conquered it yet, but I know it is possible. It's simply a matter of finding the right combination for me.*

Steps in the personal scientist approach. The personal scientist is someone who is continually "tinkering" with his behavior and fine tuning his life. He follows a series of steps (outlined below) in making repeated self-improvement effort. Once one problem is solved, he goes on to another. As with the scientist, his underlying motive is the belief that things can always be made better, new things can be learned, and one's life can be improved.

Step 1: Define the general problem area. This is essentially an "armchair analysis" of what the problem(s) might be in one's life at the moment. *I am not as happy and/or productive as I might be, but why? I feel a lot of stress or pressure from within* (probably including headaches, stomach problems, or other physical symptoms), *but why?* In answering such questions, we need to insure that the conclusions we reach are personal and not "other" oriented. You might be tempted to conclude that you are not as happy and/or productive as you might be because of the behavior of a spouse or of children, or because of some situation you face. In light of concepts presented earlier, such is not the case. You will be able to identify an effective plan for improvement only when *you* accept responsibility for how you feel and for how productive you are.

Step 2: Collect data. Once you have an idea regarding what needs to be done to improve your life, research usually is necessary in order to accurately define the problem. Research also provides a base level of performance against which to evaluate the results of your self-improvement effort. In an earlier example, Fred and Ann decided that they had a stress problem (step 1). They then recorded their stress levels for a two-week period, including situations and thoughts related to the stress (step 2). The information collected helped them to better understand the nature of the problem (step 3) and gave them some basis for determining whether their stress reduction program was effective (step 5).

If one's problem is excessive guilt, it is important to record when those feelings arise, under what circumstances, and in connection with what thoughts. Force language or "I have to's" (chapter 4) can be a problem. Again, it is useful to determine the extent to which such language is used and the circumstances in which it is used. If smoking is the problem, how many cigarettes do you smoke, and when do you smoke them? If being overweight is the problem, how much do you eat, what do you eat, and where do you eat it?

Data collection strategies are suggested in connection with some of the exercises described in the next chapter. In general, any self-improvement effort usually can be measured. If not, the goal is too ambiguous and you probably will not make much progress toward it anyway. Suppose, for example, that your goal is to be more charitable. Charity must then be defined in such a manner that you can recognize what is and what is not a charitable act. Once it is defined, you can then record the incidence of such acts over a given period of time and work out plans to increase your level of charity.

Step 3: Develop an improvement strategy. With a better understanding of the problem (gained through analyzing the research in step 2), one can then create a plan for improvement. The idea is to analyze the information collected, looking for patterns or indications of what might relieve the problem. Fred, in chapter 5, decided to leave for work or home five minutes earlier than normal and to save the last fifteen minutes of his commute for listening to music and for doing nonstress thinking. Ann came up with several procedures, also described in chapter 5, for handling the stress she was feeling.

Once you have some facts about a problem, careful and prayerful consideration normally will provide you with several ideas about how to reduce or eliminate the difficulty. Your plan needs to be realistic and practical, and it should correspond with the nature of the problem identified by your research. To illustrate, assume that you find yourself feeling responsible to make your spouse happy (rather than simply feeling responsible to be a kind, reasonable partner). As indicated in chapter 2, resentment toward spouse and considerable frustration and anger are likely to arise if you accept responsibility for how your spouse feels.

Your research indicates that the tendency to feel responsible is worse in the evenings and on weekends and holidays — when your spouse presses you to do things his or her way. It would not be practical to avoid your spouse at those critical times. It might make sense, however, to memorize a list of helpful concepts and to repeat them to yourself several times during the period when you are most likely to have a problem. Such concepts might include:

I cannot make my spouse happy. He/she is responsible for that.

My goal is to be a kind, reasonable partner.

I will say no when he/she makes unreasonable demands, *but* I will give at other times.

I can tolerate whatever manipulations I get from my spouse when I don't respond to his/her demands.

By my ignoring manipulations, his/her demands will get worse at first, but then they likely will disappear.

Having such thoughts close to the surface and ready to use increases the probability that you will reach your goal.

Step 4: Implement the plan. It is often easier to plan for improvement than to work the plan. This is especially true if the plan is unrealistic or off base. In the example just given, the plan is to memorize and repeat a few key concepts. The plan is not to get your spouse to do something (beyond your control), and it is not to avoid negative feelings toward your spouse (probably unrealistic at this point and not specifically directed at the thinking that is causing the problem). In general, if you have a problem doing what you have decided to do, this is a clue that either the plan is unrealistic or that you have a more basic problem (namely, procrastination) that needs to be resolved first (see chapter 6).

Step 5: Revise your plan if necessary. After the plan has been implemented for a while, data collection needs to be repeated. If your life has improved satisfactorily (less stress, fewer criticisms, less guilt, etc.), then you have found a suitable answer to the problem. If not, steps three and four need to be repeated, while you keep hope alive that there is an answer for you — that it just hasn't been found yet. Remember, also, that a self-improvement effort generally involves a step backward for every few steps forward.

Let me repeat a word of caution given earlier; many self-improvement goals of the type recommended in this book directly influence relationships with others. Others sometimes have an investment in old neurotic patterns, and they get upset if you refuse to play old games. In my experience, relationships almost invariably improve if goals of the type suggested here are reached; but often during an adjustment period things break loose and the original situation may worsen temporarily before it gets better. The key to evaluating the appropriateness of your efforts lies in how *you* feel about it and in how it affects *your* behavior, not in how others let themselves be affected by what you are doing.

Make the Theory Practical

The personal scientist is someone having faith in his ability to learn how to control himself. By theorizing, collecting data, experimenting, and evaluating, each of us can learn a great deal about how he personally operates. And we can develop that sometimes elusive skill of self-control. Once we are aware of our problems and are convinced that we can and will change our behavior, we are on the road to self-mastery. This doesn't mean we can eliminate all problems, but we can lead more productive lives. And we will find that our ability to cope with problems increases.

9 Emotional Control Exercises

The exercises in this chapter can help you to internalize the concepts suggested in previous chapters. And, as indicated earlier, once productive concepts are internalized they will control your feelings and behavior as certainly as did the old, less productive ideas. The exercises below also relate to steps 2 and 3 of the personal scientist approach described in chapter 8. Once you have selected a self-improvement goal, one or more of these exercises may help you to achieve your purpose.

Concept Indoctrination

Previous arguments I made support the assumption that how we feel is determined by what we think. Sometimes, of course, our perceptions and/or concepts are mistaken, which causes us to have unproductive and uncomfortable feelings. The following statements represent basic concepts presented in this book. Read each statement and circle whether you agree (A) or disagree (D).

A D Perfection need not be achieved immediately (chapter 1).

A D I need not be perfect in everything (chapter 1).

A D Mistakes are to be learned from, not feared (chapter 1).

A D Becoming perfect does not require immediately perfectionistic goals and/or great pressure on oneself to perform (chapter 1).

A D I am responsible only for that which I can control (chapter 2).

A D I can put forth an acceptable effort as a spouse or parent and still lose my marriage or children (chapter 2).

A D I can choose to feel the way I want to feel (chapter 3).

A D I can accept myself even though I feel a lack of love and respect from some people (chapter 3).

A D The way I act does not necessarily tell me what kind of person I am (chapter 3).

A D Almost nothing I face in life is terrible or awful (chapter 3).

A D Perfection is a step-by-step process in which mistakes are necessary (chapter 3).

A D I do not need to receive fair and equitable treatment from the world in order to be happy (chapter 3).

A D I can be happier in the longrun by facing life's difficulties head-on (chapter 3).

A D Self-blame is always counterproductive (chapter 4).

A D Force or power words trap us into feeling a certain way (chapter 4).

A D It makes no sense to feel guilty about feeling guilty (chapter 4).

A D Faith in God can be stress-reducing (chapter 5).

A D Worry is the most senseless source of stress there is (chapter 5).

A D Many stress points in life can be easily eliminated (chapter 5).

A D Nothing worth having can be had only at the expense of someone else (chapter 6).

A D Most jobs do not have to be done to perfection to be done satisfactorily (chapter 6).

A D Being a double victim makes no sense at all (chapter 6).

A D I can tolerate almost anything (chapter 6).

A D Long-term gain often requires short-term pain (chapter 6).

A D I can be both assertive and Christian at the same time (chapter 7).

A D Reasonable assertiveness is necessary to effective living (chapter 7).

A D Effective assertiveness requires kindness, forthrightness, and courage (chapter 7).

Now, go back and consider again the concepts with which you disagree. Chapter numbers indicate where a discussion of the concept can be found. Reread the chapters in question, think about them, pray about them, and see if you can become comfortable with the concepts. In my experience, these statements are true. And when we internalize and live by them, we can remove a great number of problems from our lives.

As a third step, review each statement and identify those you agree with but don't seem to consistently uphold. You may agree, for example, that reasonable assertiveness is necessary to effective living, but you may have great difficulty in actually asserting yourself. Make a list of the concepts you agree to but do not live by, memorize the list, and review it daily for two weeks. Then place the list in a calendar that you frequently refer to, and remind yourself of these concepts on a monthly basis for one year.

Simply reminding yourself of these ideas on a regular basis will increase the probability that your behavior will conform to the concepts. Regular reminders will also help you identify important self-improvement goals which can be worked on by using other exercises suggested below.

Thought-control, Emotion-control Exercise

The five-step exercise below (also illustrated in chapter 3) can help you solve two different types of problems: (1) when you don't feel the way that you would like to feel in given situations; and (2) when you are having trouble living by a concept you believe in.

Problem:

Describe in the above space an instance in which you felt angry, depressed, anxious, or otherwise upset, or in which your behavior did not conform to a goal you had set for yourself. For example, you may have decided that you should say no more often to unofficial service requests, but you said yes again in a situation that compromises more important priorities. Follow steps one through five below:

Step 1: What was I thinking that caused me to feel or act in that way?

1.
2.
3.
4.
5.
6.

Identify six thoughts that you remember having in the situation. If you don't remember six thoughts, fill in by guessing what you must have been thinking to cause you to feel or act the way you did.

Step 2: Why do those thoughts bother me?
1.
2.
3.
4.
5.
6.

This is a "so what?" question designed to discover troublesome thoughts not obvious on the surface. If, for example, you say yes when you should say no, you might identify one of the thoughts in step 1 as, *Sister Smith will think I am lazy or not committed to the gospel if I say no*. In step 2, the question would be, *So what? Why does that bother me?* A possible answer might be, *Because I can't be happy with myself if Sister Smith thinks that about me*. The latter statement would be recorded under step 2 above. The other five thoughts identified during step 1 would then be treated in a similar fashion.

Step 3: Are the thoughts identified during steps 1 and 2 rational? Go back to the thoughts that you have written down and determine whether they are rational. Mark those thoughts that are not rational. A thought is not rational if it (1) is incorrect, or (2) stands between you and your goal. Both of the statements in the above example are not rational. It is incorrect to say that Sister Smith *will* think I am lazy or not committed to the gospel if I say no. Sister Smith *may* feel that way, but there is no certain evidence that she will react in that manner.

In light of concepts discussed earlier, no one's happiness depends on someone else believing or doing anything. The statement *I can't be happy with myself if Sister Smith thinks that about me* is therefore incorrect. Both statements lead to saying yes, when no is the goal in this case. Both thoughts are irrational on the grounds that they hold a person back from his desired behavior.

Step 4: Rewrite the irrational thoughts into several more productive conclusions.
1.
2.

3.
4.
5.

In the spaces above, reword the thoughts that were identified as irrational in step 3. Five numbers are given, but the actual number of ideas you record will vary with your situation. The statements must be changed in a manner that makes them correct and supportive of one's improvement goal. For the two statements given, the rewrite might be done as follows: *Sister Smith may think I am lazy or uncommitted, but I really doubt that she will. Even if she does, I do not need her approval in order to be happy with myself. Both I and the Lord know I am doing the best I can, and that's all that is really important.*

Step 5: Internalize the new way of thinking. Memorize the list of new thoughts and repeat them to yourself, out loud where possible, frequently over the next few days (twenty to thirty times a day).

By frequently repeating the above exercise in many different situations, you will develop a habit of thinking rationally. When you reach that point, the exercise can be discontinued. Until then, following the procedure step by step is important. It is particularly critical that the procedure be completed in writing. Simply trying to think oneself through the exercise usually will not work.

Quasi-Stationary Equilibrium Exercise

The quasi-stationary equilibrium exercise is of value in defining subgoals in connection with efforts to improve one's performance. As indicated in chapter 1, you often can more effectively improve your performance by removing obstacles to accomplishment than by putting pressure on yourself to perform.

Assume that you have come to the conclusion that you want to expand your social base and to reach out to new people. According to the personal scientist approach, it then would be necessary to collect as much information as possible about your current social life. This could be done by —

1. writing down the names of everyone you consider to be a friend, differentiating between surface and close friendships;
2. identifying the amount of time you spent with each person on the list in the last month (distinguish between group and one-on-one interactions);
3. recording your thoughts and feelings immediately after social encounters over a one- to two-week period.

Using the information collected, identify factors which lead to expanding contacts with other people as well as factors which inhibit social activity. Then record the factors identified, as illustrated below.

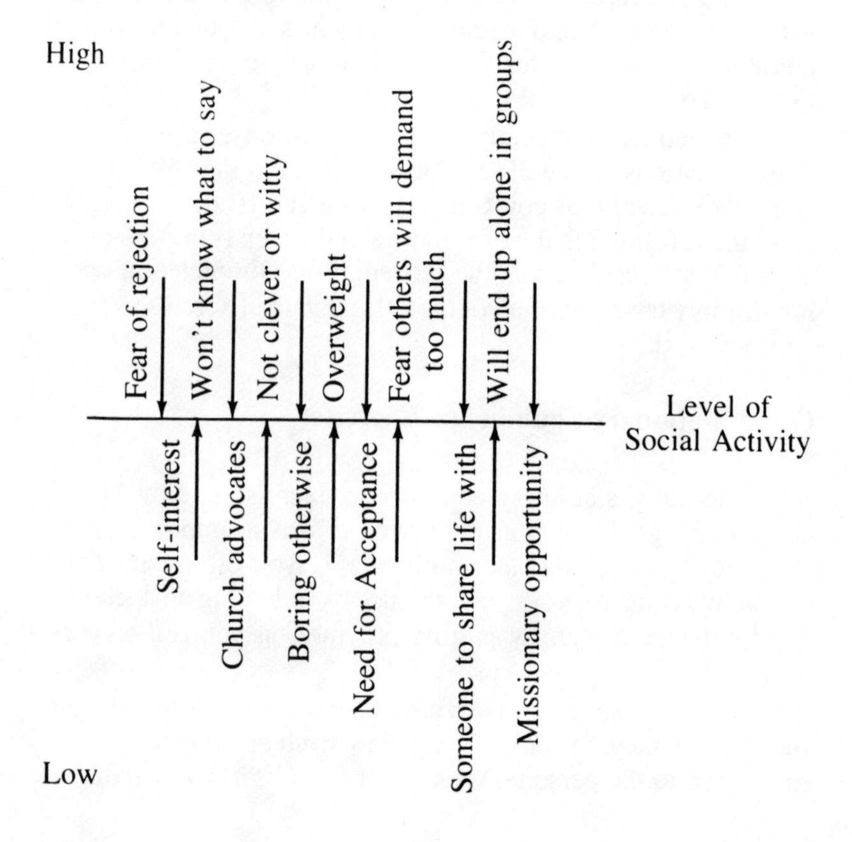

The goal would then be to eliminate or reduce each factor on top of the achievement line. Simply putting pressure on oneself to be more sociable probably would be ineffective in the long run. The approach outlined above, however, identifies a series of specific subgoals that need to be addressed in connection with the overall goal of increasing social activity. Working on the subgoals one at a time will lead to success with the overall goal.

To start using this technique, select an achievement goal and identify positive and negative forces influencing the outcome. Write the factors in the figure below.

Goal:

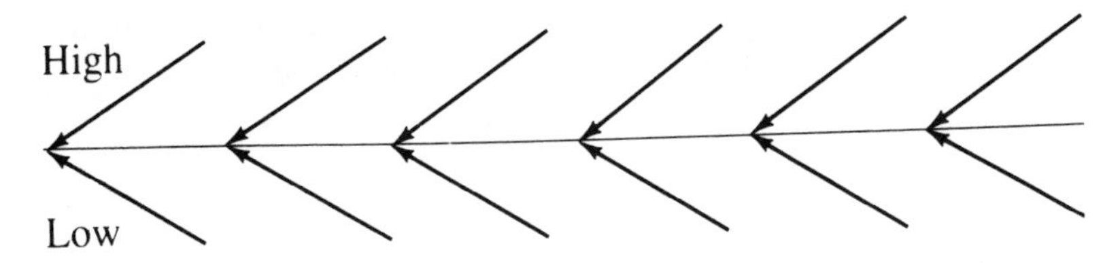

Having completed the figure, you now have identified a number of subgoals necessary in reaching your overall objective. You can then make specific plans for reducing or eliminating each obstacle to the performance you desire.

Stress-Cataloging Exercise

I recommend that you try the exercise described in chapter 5. Stress problems are extremely common in today's high-pressure society. It is possible that you are suffering negative effects from stress, even though you have accommodated yourself to the point that you don't recognize the problem.

For a complete stress-cataloging review, go back to chapter 5 and follow the steps outlined there. Short of that, you may wish to take a few moments now to complete a rudimentary analysis of stress points in your life by filling in information under the headings given below.

What have I worried most about during the last week? (Write down *all* ideas that come to mind.)

What bothers me most about my past? (Are there things from the past that you still feel guilty about ?)

Who have I been in a negative confrontation with in the last month? What was the confrontation about?

What might happen in the next five years that I worry most about?

What should I be doing now that I am not doing? (This could be a long list. Remember to include everyday chores as well as more significant concerns.)

If you carefully answer the preceding questions you will almost certainly reveal a great number of pressure points in your life. The next step is to go back over the stress sources identified and to see which items could be quickly eliminated. Often something as simple as changing your daily schedule, completing a procrastinated task, deciding that something need not be done after all, talking to the bishop about something you still feel guilty about, or expressing your feelings to someone will remove a stress point. Other sources of stress are more difficult to overcome, but they usually are not impossible to reduce or eliminate. Generally, it helps just to think about things differently.

Relaxation Exercise

Sometimes a brief time-out from stress is useful. The exercise recommended below may not alleviate problems directly; but the "breather" it provides can recharge one's battery. The exercise therefore can be especially helpful when coping capacity seems to be temporarily depleted.

The objective of the exercise is to spend ten minutes focusing on total body relaxation and away from troublesome, stress-inducing thoughts. It is helpful but not necessary to complete the exercise in a quiet place. It can be completed sitting up or lying down; although by lying down you may get so comfortable that you fall asleep.

I recommend that you record the following or a similar dialogue on tape (the specific words you use are not that important). Listening to the tape is usually more relaxing than reading the dialogue or talking yourself through it, which also are options if a tape recorder is not available.

Sample dialogue

"My objective in the next ten minutes is to totally relax. I will begin by fixing my eyes on the corner of the ceiling where the walls come together. Count to five and close my eyes. One — two — three — four — five. Eyes closed. I am beginning to relax. I will take three very deep breaths, and as I exhale I will repeat in my mind the word *relax*. My total purpose for the moment is relaxation. Any noises I hear will not disturb me, but will simply be a signal to relax even more. I must concentrate on what I am doing and on the sound of my voice. I will follow my instructions exactly. Now, breathing in — deeply — exhale — repeating the word *relax*. Again — deeply — relax. Once more — deeply — relax.

"I will now tense the muscles in my forehead and squeeze my eyelids tightly, maintaining the pressure until it hurts — hold it — now relax. Let a feeling of relief fill the muscles around my eyes and forehead. Again — tense and release. Now I will press my chin tightly to my chest and raise my shoulders, again squeezing until it hurts — hold it — relax. Let my shoulders drop and the muscles in my neck go limp. A feeling of peace is beginning to be felt in my body. Now I will make fists and tighten the muscles in my arms until they hurt — hold it — relax. A calming, soothing, feeling is now in my hands and arms. Now I will tense the muscles in my legs and curl my toes — tightly — hold it — now release. Again, a feeling of peace and calm — total relaxation in my legs. Now I will tense my whole body. Go ahead — eyelids, chin, shoulders, hands, arms, legs, toes — hold it — relax. Think calm. Think peace. Think freedom. Now again. Total body tension. Hold it longer this time. Hold it. Now relax. Deeper, deeply into relaxation.

"My scalp is relaxed, jaw loose and relaxed, facial muscles relaxed, neck and shoulders relaxed — at ease. Chest muscles relaxed. Muscles in the back are loose. Let them go. Hip and abdominal muscles, legs and toes are loose, relaxed. Stress and strain are leaving the body, out through the finger-tips, out through the toes. The whole body now feels limp, heavy, relaxed. So very — very — comfortable. Stress and strain are draining out of the body and being replaced by a warm, heavy feeling beginning at the top of the head and moving down through the body. Over and over — top of the head and down through the body. Over and over — top of the head and down through the body.

"Relax and let go. Let down — deeper and deeper.

Counting now from one to ten — with each count sinking, drifting, deeper and deeper. One — deeper, two — relax, three — down, four — relax, five — let go, six — deeper and deeper. Seven — going down, eight — at ease, nine — very deep, ten — at total rest. Very, very peaceful. All is calm, all is relaxed, deeply, heavily relaxed.

"Now that I am relaxed, my mind is free and clear to meditate. I will imagine myself lying on a deserted, warm beach — no pain, no care — totally relaxed, hearing the sound of the waves, feeling the warmth of the sun. I smell the salt air. No one is around. I am totally at peace. No demands. Warmth — peace — total relaxation. Remembering now that I am a child of God, *a child of God*. He loves me and will help me do right. All will be right if I serve him. As I serve him, all things will work for my good. I am a person of worth and value. I can accomplish my reasonable goals.

"Now when I count to five, I will be fully awake and alert, feeling comfortable, alive, relaxed, ready for the day. One — two — three — four [louder] five — wide awake and alert, eyes open."

As you record the dialogue remember that the exact wording is not critical. Change the dialogue to better represent your personal vocabulary and feelings. You may also wish to change the relaxation image. The beach works for me, but you may be able to invent a more pleasant thought for you. This period of relaxation can also be used to remind yourself of your goals. Such self-talk seems to have more impact when you repeat it while you're relaxed.

The quality of your voice is not a critical factor, but it is helpful to speak in mellow, soothing, and relaxed tones. You should speak slowly, giving yourself sufficient time to follow each directive. This exercise can be used as often as time and interest allow. Some make it a daily practice, while others use it only at times of high stress.

Emotive-Imagery Exercise

We so often avoid difficult emotional situations that we don't get much actual practice in handling them effectively; sometimes we are so locked into certain behavioral responses that it is very difficult to change our approach at the time of emotional stress. But we can practice emotional control in the privacy (and safety) of our own minds and, thereby, prepare ourselves to be more effective in actual situations.

Pick a recent negative confrontation with someone in your life — spouse, child, friend, employer, acquaintance — and replay it in your mind. Try to visualize the scene in as much detail as possible, as if you were watching it on television. What was the other person(s) wearing? Visualize the setting in detail. What was the other person saying. Visualize his or her countenance and body movements. Look at yourself in equal detail. Fill in details missing from your memory, but try to relive the actual situation. If your visualization is effective, you will begin to feel the same way you did during the actual confrontation.

Once your emotions are involved, press yourself to move from being highly agitated to being disappointed or concerned. Keep the details of the situation vivid, but make your emotional response more moderate. What are you thinking? What are you saying? How do you look as you move from intense to minimum emotion? Notice that in order to move toward less emotion you must change what you are thinking about the situation. Try to identify the more moderate thinking and remember it as you play the situation out in your mind.

This technique works, as suggested above, after the fact. It can also be of value before intended confrontation. Suppose that you expect an encounter with a supervisor or loved one. Imagine the situation in detail. Visualize the worst possible outcome — the most negative consequence and behavior from the other person. Also imagine yourself handling the negative encounter with disappointment or concern, but not with exceptional emotion. What are you thinking that lets you handle the situation in a relatively relaxed manner? Work with the image until you can handle it with minimum discomfort.

Although it is not necessary to do so, it sometimes can be of value to employ the imagery exercise suggested here in connection with the preceding relaxation exercise. In that case, you would do your emotional control practice after getting yourself totally relaxed. The advantage of this is that vivid visualization and concentration sometimes are easier to create when you are completely relaxed.

How often should you practice? As much and as often as possible until you are able to handle difficult situations effectively.

Worst-Outcome Exercise

The idea of the worst-outcome exercise is to imagine the worst possible outcome in a feared situation and then to work with that fear until it is no longer a worry. I suggest three levels of attack in working with the fear. At the first level, write down all the reasons why you have no need to fear the event. For example, assume that you are afraid of public speaking. Reasons for not fearing include:

1. People will accept me whether or not I do a great job.
2. If I do my best, the Lord will help me do the rest.
3. Everyone is in the same boat. People will understand my feelings.
4. I will not lose anything of importance (friendship, health, love, respect, spirituality) if I try and don't do a great job. But I could lose some of those things if I don't try.
5. What I will be doing is not that much different from general conversation, and I am not afraid to talk to people.

These and other reasons should be memorized and repeated to oneself frequently.

Then go on to the second level. In as much detail as possible, imagine yourself speaking in public. Start by visualizing yourself being introduced, then standing in front of a specific group, and finally speaking. If you do not become emotionally intense during the visualization, focus your image and include more detail. Visualize the people in the audience. What are they wearing? What are they doing? What are they thinking? Once you are emotionally involved, work with the image until you can imagine yourself speaking comfortably before the group.

You can start the third phase, actually speaking in public, by forcing yourself to give answers or to ask questions in a class you attend. Move from that point to volunteering to pray or to give a brief presentation before the group. You will then be ready to volunteer for a formal speech.

Self-reinforcement

Even after following the three steps suggested above, it is sometimes so difficult to volunteer for a public speech or to complete some other self-improvement goal that you need an external incentive to get yourself moving. Often, too, a reward can help us sustain our efforts on desirable but uncomfortable activities, such as losing weight, studying, or completing some long-procrastinated task.

Identify something very pleasant but infrequently enjoyed, and make doing or having that thing contingent upon completing some task. You may, for example, enjoy listening to music but hate studying. You could, in that case, reinforce studying by following it with music. You might set up the following plan: *For every forty-five minutes of study time, I will reward myself with fifteen minutes of listening to my favorite albums.*

A few criteria for a successful self-reinforcement program include the following:

1. The reward must be rewarding. If you promise yourself a gift but then feel guilty about receiving it, or if it is not something you really enjoy, it will lose its value as a reinforcer.
2. Place the reinforcement soon after the difficult activity. Rewarding a teenager with a new car for successful grades in high school can be effective, but often the reward promised is too distant for it to have an impact on studying on any given night. Lesser, more immediate rewards, such as listening to music after study time, are often more effective.
3. Don't hesitate to use verbal reinforcement on yourself. Some of us are taught that only a proud individual would compliment himself. In my experience, those who can effectively compliment themselves (privately) for a job well done gain the strength needed to be humble. Self-critical people are often stubborn, hardheaded, and, in a word, proud.
4. Make certain that the activity to be rewarded is clearly defined. Keeping one's temper, being more charitable or loving, and being a better spouse are examples of ambiguous goals. It is necessary to define each objective so explicitly that it is obvious when the goal has been achieved.
5. Expect only a reasonable amount of effort before giving yourself the reward. Five hours of study in exchange for fifteen minutes of music probably won't work. Like overall goals, subgoals need to be realistic and practical.

The essence of the message of this book is that most of us unnecessarily complicate our lifes, that by ineffective coping responses we often compound problems that come to us, in effect, creating problems where none would otherwise exist. Lehi's words, "men are, that they might have joy" (2 Nephi 2:25), are a constant reminder to us that we can be happy. But the equally important message is one of hope. We need not continue to make things extra difficult for ourselves. Of course, it is not possible to remove all problems from life; that would counter our purpose for being here. But it is possible to live much more comfortably than we sometimes do; and, not incidentally, it is possible to live more productively as well.

Index

— A —

Accountability, 95-96
Achievement, 76, 83
Adam and Eve, 11
Adultery, 48-51
Alma, 48
Anger, 2-4, 28-29, 31, 59, 77-78, 85
Anxiety, 54, 57
Arguments, 83
Assertiveness, 89-102
Assignments, completion of, 54-55, 80. *See also* Callings
Attention, 91-92
Attitude, control of, 5, 31, 38
Authority figures, 97
Automobile, accidents, 26, 34
 driving, 42-45, 62-63

— B —

Behavior, changeableness of, 49
 insensitive, 40
 of children, 33-34
 of others, 25
Bishops, 14
Bitterness, 51
Blame. *See* Self-condemnation

— C —

Callings, performance in, 19-22, 77, 94-95
Caring. *See* Loving
Celestial kingdom, 83
Children, problems with, 2, 21-23
 value of, 33-34
Church assignments. *See* Callings
Church membership, 103
Circumstances, 81, 84
Civility, 98
Commitments, 95
Communication, 99
Competition, 83
Complaints, 56, 98
Compliments, 91-92
Conference. *See* General Conference
Confidence, 13, 101
Conformity, 27
Confrontation, 101
Consistency, 88
Control, of others, 27
 of self, 31, 45, 106-7
Cookery, 10
Coping skills, 1
Courage, 100
Crises, 55
Criticism, 56, 67, 92, 98. *See also* Self-condemnation

— D —

Data collection strategies, 108
Deadlines, 55
Defensiveness, 92
Demands, unreasonable, 97-98

Depression, 60
  perfection-oriented, 8, 13
  situations, 2
Destiny, eternal, 1
Dialogue, with self, 50, 54
Dieting, 38, 77, 88, 108
Discomfort, 97
Disruptions, 93
Divorce, 23-24, 30
"Double victims," 52, 67, 85
Down times. *See* Depression
Dread, 68

— E —

Ecclesiastical courts, 99
Education Week, 8
Emotional responses, 14
Emotions, control of, 31, 38-45, 59
  definition of, 28
  exercises for control of, 112-28
Equality, 37
Eternal destiny, 1
Example, 25
Excommunicated people, 48-51
Exercise, 87
Extremism, 104, 105

— F —

Failure, 15-16, 101
Fairness, 37
Faith, lack of, 17
Family home evenings. *See* Home evenings
Fathers, 21-22
Favors, requests for, 95
Fear, 17, 69, 100
Feelings, bad, 59
  of others, 25
Finance, personal, 51-52
Food additives, 5
Food supply, 68
Force language, 54-58, 108
Forgiveness, 53-54
Former members, 48-51
Forthrightness, 99
Friends, 118
Frustration, 2, 78, 86
Future, concern about, 69

— G —

General Conference, 8
Goals, attainment of, 8, 86
  selection of, 9
God, agency of, 27
  anger with, 49, 78
  emotions of, 45
Good works, 17
Gospel principles, standard of, 14
Gourmet cookery, 10
Gratification, 86
Guilt, 4, 26, 104, 108
  appropriateness of, 8, 48-49
  interpretation of, 60
  unnecessary, 46-47

— H —

Habits, 14-15
Happiness, 37-38, 83, 84
Health, and stress, 61
Hedonism, 86
Hermits, 11
Home evenings, 106
Homemaking, 2-3, 71
  perfection in, 10, 77, 84-85
Homework, 76
Hopelessness, 49
Hostility. *See* Anger
Husband-wife relationship, 3, 24, 39-42, 57, 58, 78, 93-94, 99, 109
Hypoglycemia, 5

— I —

Imagery exercises, 124-25
Imagination, 71
Impatience, 2
Improvement. *See* Self-improvement
Inconvenience, 93
Inertia, 88
Insensitivity, 40

Interruptions, 91
Intruders, 70
Investment management, 51-52
Irritations, 97

— J —

Jesus Christ, assertiveness of, 90
perfection of, 9-10
Jobs. *See* Work
Judgment, 37

— K —

Kindness, 98

— L —

Latter-day Saints, character of, 7
Laziness, 75. *See also* Procrastination
Learning, vicarious, 11-12
Life, problems in, 1, 38
Love, addicts, 91-92
expressing, 92-93
in marriage, 58, 65-66, 93-94
incapacity for, 33
need for, 55
Loving, problems in, 5

— M —

McGregor, Douglas, on management, 16-17
Management, theories of, 16-17
Marriage, 23-24, 93-94
Mediocrity, 10
Menstrual cycles, 5
Missionaries, and parents, 25-26
Missionary work, 78
Mistakes, 11, 12, 59
Moderation, 104
Moods, 81
Mormons. *See* Latter-day Saints
Mortality, pre-mortal expectations of, 1
Mothers, 2-3
Motivation, 81
Musical instruments, 7-8

— N —

Needs, satisfaction of, 55
Noninvolvement, 100
Nonverbal communication, 99

— O —

Offense, 30
Opinions, 31
Opportunity, 81-82
Overprotection, 21
Overreaction, 4, 13

— P —

Parents, forceful, 58
influence, 21-23
responsibility, 26
Passivity, 100
Patience, 88, 101
Perception, 29, 57
Perfection, and mistakes, 11, 12
in scripture, 35
misperceptions of, 7-15
standards of, 13
Personality, development of, 33-34
Physiology, and emotions, 5
Plans, 93
Practice, 7-8, 59
Pressure, parental, 58
work-related, 16, 79-80
Problems, definition of, 107
solving, 106-10
universality of, 1, 19
Procrastination, 10
overcoming, 82-88
reasons given for, 74-78
Productivity, and stress, 61, 73
Progress, 59, 88
Projects. *See* Work
Punctuality, 39
Punishment, 87

— Q —

Quasi-Stationary equilibrium, 17, 57, 117-19

— R —

"Railroad tie" view, 59
Rationalization, 79-82
Reactions, of others, 13-14
Rebellion, 58
Recreation, 83
Regret, 4
Reinforcement. *See* Rewards
Rejection, 100
Relaxation, 62, 72, 121-23
Relaxed perspectives, 57
Reminders, 88
Repentance, 12-13, 35
Resolve, 98
Responsibility, 24-27, 36, 95, 96
  personal, 36-37
Rewards, 87, 126-27

— S —

Sacrament meeting, 106
Security, 83
Self-condemnation, 10, 12, 17, 47, 49, 75, 88
Self-control. *See* Control
Self-esteem, 83
Self-fulfilling prophecy, 57
Self-improvement, 9, 18, 88, 104, 108, 110
Self-mastery, 93
Self-reinforcement. *See* Rewards
Self-respect, 2, 13
Self-talk, 50, 123
Self-worth, 84
Sensitivity, 40
Service, requests for, 95
Shoplifting, 33
Sill, Sterling W., on emotions, 32
Sin, 35
Situations, nature of, 29, 34
Smoking, 15, 96, 108
Social conduct, 13-14, 118
Sorrow, 60
Spite. *See* Vengeance
Stake conference, 9
Status, 83, 84
Stealing, 33
Stewardship. *See* Accountability
Stress, 108
  cataloging, 63-67, 119-21
  monitoring, 62-63
  reactions to, 61-62
  unnecessary, 68-71
Study habits, 76, 126-27

— T —

Talents, 10
Tardiness, 39
Temper. *See* Anger
Tension. *See* Stress
Thought, control of, 30-31, 38-39, 115-17
  detailed, 72
  for relaxation, 71
  habitual, 58
  power of, 5
  rational, 40-45, 116
Time, pressure of, 55

— U —

Unforgiveness. *See* Forgiveness
Unthoughtfulness, 39

— V —

Vengeance, 4, 85
Visualization, 71

— W —

Ward activities, 19
Weight loss. *See* Dieting
Widtsoe, John A., on fear, 69
Words, of power, 54-58
Work, excellence in, 10, 85
  situations, 13, 80-82
Works, good, 17
Worry, 70-73
Worst-possible-outcome, 70-71, 125-126